the complete guide to

Hong Kong

CFW Guidebooks
Published by CFW Publications Limited
130 Connaught Road C Hong Kong

© CFW Publications Limited, 1981
Printed in Hong Kong

PHOTO CREDITS
Maxim Caterers Ltd: Pages 70-71
The Peninsula Group Ltd: Pages 72-73, 75.

ISBN 962 7031 02 X

Contents

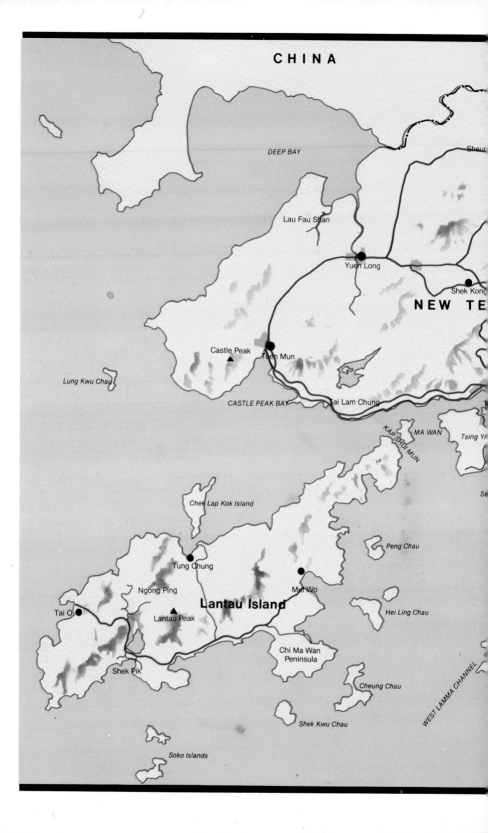

the complete guide to
Hong Kong

By Charles F Williams

Photography: Lincoln Potter

CFW GUIDEBOOKS
Hong Kong

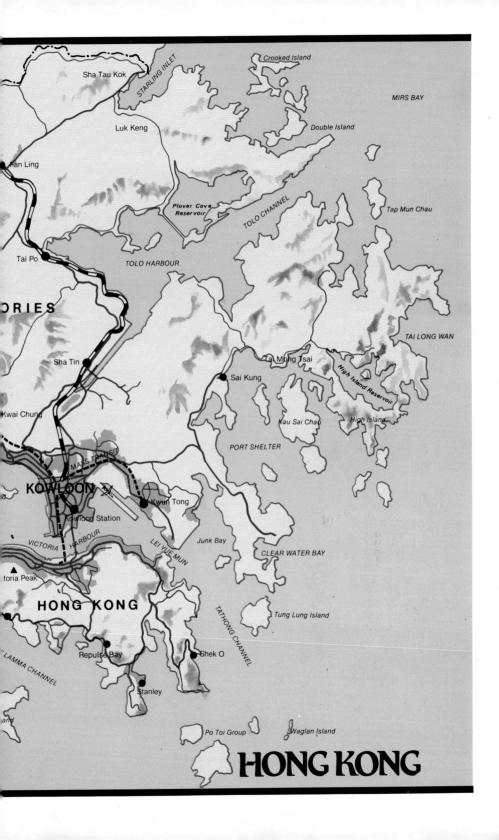

HONG KONG

An Opiated Birth
The Historical Hong Kong

The British Crown Colony of Hong Kong today prides itself in its conservatism, commercial prudence, industrial strength and a kind of old-world puritanism — which is a far cry from its swashbuckling, even bizarre, 140 years of recorded history.

It's a history of opium and piracy, political scandal, warships and gunboats blockading the China coast, a tiny territory swollen with the human and material overspill of tumultuous mainland rebellions and civil wars — of two of the world's greatest powers locked in economic conflict. It's a romantic history, to say the least, and one in which fact outshines fiction enough to produce a story alongside which the most outrageous Hollywood scenario would tend to pale.

That was certainly the story of Hong Kong as it began in the imperial 19th century. Before that, for thousands of years previously, Hong Kong Island and its mainland territory and surrounding cluster of isles were hardly worth a second look. A number of rock carvings on one of these islands show that the area was uninhabited right up until the 14th century, when the first small groups of mainland settlers crossed what is now Victoria Harbour, followed a couple of centuries later by roving fleets of **Hoklos** — the "sea gypsies" of southern China. It wasn't until the late 18th century that semi-permanent settlements of fishing people and pirates were established in the sheltered bays of what are now **Shaukiwan** and **Aberdeen**.

It wasn't until the early 19th century, and the rather tragi-comic struggle that developed between aggressive British traders and the imperious Ch'ing dynasty rulers of China, that Hong Kong assumed physical and political significance.

Even then, when it was finally taken as a prize of war in 1841, the British in Whitehall — and Queen Victoria herself — ridiculed it as a worthless rocky landfall. But Hong Kong had something of value that the "China traders" were willing to fight their own government for. It had the finest and safest deepwater port on the whole China coast; better still, this prized anchorage and adjacent island were sufficiently removed from Chinese control to guarantee security from conflict that was disrupting trade in the mainland Treaty Ports. And it was this security as an offshore trading depot that transformed Hong Kong from a "barren lump of rock" to the wealthy emporium and industrial centre that it is today.

The sires of this unlikely birth were enterprising, often scurrilous, "Merchant Princes" — freebooting British merchant seaman who, by 1833, had inherited the old East India Company's trading power in Southeast Asia and coastal China. But they also inherited a longstanding and bitter struggle to force China to actually engage in trade. For many years, fierce British trading assaults had been blunted by successive Chinese emperors who wanted nothing to do with the British or their products. China was omnipotent and self-sufficient, didn't trust the British — or any other European adventurers, for that matter, except the Portuguese Jesuits — and was willing to give up its coveted teas and silks only for hard cash, and certainly not the products of Britain's Industrial Revolution.

On the British side, this Chinese intransigence produced a dangerous trading deficit. From the 17th to mid-19th centuries, Britain purchased an average of four million silver taels' worth of tea (one tael equals 38 grams) from China each year. But the amount of British goods taken in exchange — wool, cotton and metals — was less than one-sixth that total; and this meant that Britain's silver bullion reserves were dipping dangerously low to pay for Chinese tea. Between 1786 and 1829 the

British East Indiamen and trading barques made eight trading expeditions to China loaded down with cotton textiles. They barely managed to recover their costs. Three British political delegations went to China to demand, through diplomacy and threats, that trading facilities be widened and more respect be shown for the marvels of Britain's factories and mills. They were all quite unceremoniously turned down.

The British needed Chinese tea, Chinese silks — even Chinese rhubarb, for medicinal purposes. China required nothing of Britain except her silver. The British cast frantically about for something, *anything*, that would tempt China into a more equitable form of trade. And they finally came up with one trading commodity that the Chinese apparently couldn't refuse — opium.

Opium came from British-administered India, where farmers had been growing it for centuries, mainly for their own use. Opium had also been used in China, largely as a medicine, but up until 1767 it had hardly taken hold beyond the herbal medic's shelf, and annual imports had been less than 200 chests a year. By 1800, the Bengali poppy plantations were working overtime for export, the British were shipping no less than 2,000 chests of opium a year into China through Canton, smuggling the nefarious stuff in and bribing Chinese officials as they went. With profits as high as $1,000 a chest, there was no way in which the "Merchant Princes" could be restrained. American smugglers joined the British, competing with their swift, newly-developed trading Clippers. By 1830, the flood of opium into China had reached 10,000 chests a year, and it rose to 40,000 eight years later.

In what must rank as one of the most infamous conflicts of history, two national addictions were now at war with each other. The British craving for tea had all but emptied the silver reserves of the British Treasury. Now, in a Chinese society well and truly hooked on opium, with an estimated two million addicts by 1835 embracing almost every social class, the silver flow was reversed — it was now the Chinese themselves who were alarmed at the rapidly falling level of their own bullion reserves.

The outcome of this confrontation was more conflict, and on a more violent level — and the rather grudging, uncelebrated birth of Hong Kong.

The Chinese Emperor, angered by the crippling outflow of Chinese silver, the widespread social debilitation from opium and the audacity of the British, appointed a Commissioner for Canton, Lin Tse-hsu, to put a stop to the trade. Commissioner Lin, an honest, scholarly statesman, issued an edict in March 1839 ordering the British to surrender all their

Stately Queen Victoria still holds her place in this bustling city.

opium stocks, and his troops surrounded the British warehouses in Canton to make sure they complied. After a seige lasting six weeks, the British gave in — their Superintendent of Trade, Captain Charles Elliot, who, admittedly, was personally opposed to the opium trade, supervising the surrender of some 20,000 chests of what the Chinese contemptuously referred to as "foreign mud."

But the Chinese triumph was short-lived. Elliot withdrew the British trading community to a safe haven east of the Pearl River estuary called Heung Kong, "Fragrant Harbour" — Hong Kong. From there he was ordered to apply gunboat diplomacy against the Chinese to force them to open up to free trade, and British forces blockaded the Canton and Yangtze Rivers and threatened Peking. The emperor's response was to sack Commissioner Lin and send down another Commissioner, the Manchu Keshen, to stall the British with negotiations.

Elliot, no doubt persuaded by the merchants, demanded that the British be granted one or more of their own "sufficiently large and conveniently situated islands" from which they could trade with China without fear of physical reprisal — and chose Hong Kong. After another British show of muscle on the Canton River, Keshen agreed — and on January 25 1841 the Union Jack was raised at Possession Point, west of what is now the **Man Mo Temple** on today's **Hollywood Road**, and Hong Kong became a possession of the Crown.

And, ironic as it might seem, both Keshen and Elliot paid dearly for that agreement. Even before pen and inkbrush were put to paper, Keshan was dragged back to Peking in chains for relinquishing sovereign Chinese territory, and Elliot was called home to London in disgrace by an infuriated Foreign Secretary, Lord Palmerston, for allowing himself to be palmed off by the Chinese with a "barren piece of land with hardly a house upon it."

For the next two years, Hong Kong was more an embarrassment than a colonial possession. Whitehall literally turned its nose up at it, refusing to even allow the island to develop. It wasn't until Elliot's successor, Sir Henry Pottinger, sailed up the Yangtze, giving the Chinese a vigorous military hiding on the way, and a complicated but fairly comprehensive free trade agreement was reached, ending the so-called First Opium War, that Hong Kong was grudgingly accepted as a true possession and not a liability; and in August 1842, almost two years after the Union Jack was raised on its foreshores, Hong Kong was granted full colonial status.

The colony's official birth marked an arrangement between the British and Chinese that was part *fait accompli* and part compromise. The island was remote enough from Canton that not too many Chinese imperial feathers were ruffled — the "foreign devils" were, at least, kept at a distance. On the British side, there was very little celebration; in fact, ever since that historic date the Hong Kong authorities have diplomatically refrained from declaring an official annual celebration or public holiday to mark the colony's foundation. This sort of tacit understanding between the British and Chinese has been the hallmark of the colony's inner mechanism ever since that date.

But if China thought it had halted the barbarian threat in 1842, it was soon proved wrong. Having claimed Hong Kong Island for the Crown, the British pressed further into China's underbelly, taking advantage of a dynastic rule that was weakened by its own rigid traditions and corruption. In 1856, at the height of the Second Opium War, Whitehall retaliated for a clash between Chinese officials and British officers aboard a British ship by insisting on a second treaty giving them full diplomatic recognition in Peking. And in 1860, when a shot was fired at the first British ambassador as he was on his way to the Chinese capital, British honour

demanded yet another treaty which widened their hold on Hong Kong — giving them sovereignty over the Kowloon peninsula up to the area now marked by **Boundary Street**, and a second "lump of rock," Stonecutters Island.

In 1898, Britain expanded its colony once again, this time as a result of a competitive land-grab by all the Great Powers. The Chinese were by now bowing to Russian, American and French pressure on territory north of Boundary Street. The Russians were using port facilities in Kowloon and looking around for colonial real estate. The Americans had used **Mirs Bay** as a marshalling spot for their naval attack on The Philippines in the Spanish-American War.

Neither Russia nor America was regarded as a serious threat to British interests, but when France began seeking land in what is now the **New Territories** for a coaling station and foothold in China, Whitehall decided that things had

gone far enough. In June 1898, an agreement was signed with the Chinese giving Britain the New Territories and **Outlying Islands** of Hong Kong — an additional 934 square kilometers of sovereignty.

But unlike the previous treaties on Hong Kong Island and Kowloon, in which the land was turned over in perpetuity, this New Territories deal was a 99-year lease.

That lease runs out on June 9, 1997, and in theory the New Territories revert back to China on that date. Whether this actually happens or not remains to be seen — but in this present day and age, with Whitehall now dealing with an entirely "new" and more powerful China altogether, that date is never far from the thoughts and plans of the British administration and business community in Hong Kong.

Treasured possessions find a special place even in a modest shack.

Triumph of the Taipans
The Colonial Heritage

In 1844, when the first population figures were recorded in Hong Kong, "heathens" outnumbered "barbarians" by more than 400 to 1 — exactly 19,009 Chinese against 454 British. By the end of the century the Chinese population had burgeoned to 247,000, while the "foreigners" totalled only 14,000. And in 1980, the "foreign devils" were still very much in the minority; 98 percent of Hong Kong's population was Chinese.

It's hardly surprising then that the *hongs* — the powerful British trading houses that founded Hong Kong and, with hard-nosed *laissez faire* business principles, guided it to prosperity — are now becoming predominantly Chinese. The reins of financial power are changing hands, and have been doing so since the beginning of the 1970s — far too quickly for some of the old colonial curmudgeons who still haunt some of the boardrooms, far too slowly for the growing ranks of university-educated young Chinese who no longer see their futures pinned to China or Taiwan, or emigration. Yet in essence, in reality and maybe even in perpetuity, Hong Kong is still *quaite* British. Until China decides what to do about the crucial New Territories lease in 1997, Hong Kong will undoubtedly remain a British Crown Colony.

It will also probably retain its traditional "special relationship" not only with the powers that prevail in Peking but also with the government back home. So far as Whitehall is concerned, Hong Kong remains a possession that's still somewhat more of an embarrassment than a colonial prize — a splendid money-making machine but certainly not a society than one could blow a trumpet about in this day and age. It has no representation in British Parliament, and doesn't want it anyway; indeed, the last thing that both the Home Government and colonial bureaucracy would wish to see is Hong Kong listed for intensive parliamentary debate. It has no democracy — its governing officials appointed directly by the Governor on behalf of the Crown, with its only free electoral process confined to "ratepayers" who can vote every four years for "unofficial" representatives on the Urban Council, a sort of municipal authority responsible for things like street cleaning, hawker control and cultural events.

The colony's fantastic commercial and industrial success has been built on cheap labour, an exploitation that today's business chiefs rationalise as the only realistic means by which a trading post with no real resources of its own, except people, could hope to compete and survive in this cruel commercial world. That's probably true, but it's a tradition that's hardly complimentary to the mother country's own industrial image. You rarely read about Hong Kong in the British newspapers. It's as if Whitehall and Westminister prefer to think it doesn't actually exist at all. And that's where one facet of Hong Kong's "special relationship" shines out — it enjoys a large measure of autonomy, with little interference from home, so long as it doesn't become too much of a political and social embarrassment . . . and makes a lot of money.

These same basic principles apply to Hong Kong's special relationship with China. The same compromise and pragmatism have allowed the British to cling to this little pimple on the Chinese buffalo's backside. Though they wrested it by force from a weak, collapsing Old World order, they've managed to hold on to it in the face of Chinese Communism

and anti-imperialist sentiment by unabashedly acting as a window on to the capitalist world, a political and commercial handmaiden to the revolutionary rulers in Peking.

The compromises represent a triumph of pragmatism over imperial pride. Officially, Hong Kong must not call itself a *colony* — certainly not outside its own shores — nor a *state*, *city-state*, or, God forbid, a *nation*. It is referred to in government information as a *territory*. Major political, economic and even social decisions are made not in the inner sanctums of Whitehall but over tea in Canton and Peking. Even the colonial status is worth little more than the papers that were signed in the last century: Although British and Chinese interests have merged somewhat in the present-day *rapprochment* and modernisation of China, Peking still insists that because the People's Republic does not recognise territorial agreements made before the revolution, there's no legal reason for it to hold to the Hong Kong treaties.

In return for a little realism and the token nature of their powers, the British are free to be as British as they like amid the joss-smoke and gongs and teeming, free-wheeling rat-race of Chinese business and social life in Hong Kong. And it's this tenacity of British tradition and a sort of collision of separate cultures that gives Hong Kong its distinctive John Bull image — with its annual dog and cat shows; continuing conflict between the SPCA (Society for the Prevention of Cruelty to Animals) and the Chinese *penchant* for slaughtering and eating dogs; military tattoos; psuedo-English pubs; a flourishing Letters to the Editor page in the *South China Morning Post*; society snaps and social snobbery in the *Hong Kong Tatler*; double-decker buses; bone china, sterling silver and Home Counties twin-sets at Lane Crawford; Government House garden parties and

The Connaught Centre landmark provides a striking back-drop to the Union Jack.

the annual pilgrimage to view the Governor's prized azaleas; New Year's and Queen's Birthday Honours Lists bestowing tributes and titles upon business leaders, social lions and retiring civil servants for their distinguished services to the community. Under China's rules, as with Whitehall's, the British masquerade is sanctioned so long as Hong Kong doesn't cause any undue political embarrassment . . . and makes a lot of money. And money is something that it certainly knows how to make; on the public side alone, there are very few governments in the world today that can boast continuing surpluses of between HK$3-billion and HK$5-billion a year.

But it wasn't always that way. Hong Kong's success story took some years to build up to the proverbial rattling good yarn. In 1842 the colony was simply one of the spoils of war. India was the most glittering jewel in Queen Victoria's crown, but Hong Kong was nothing more than an anchorage and godown (warehouse) for British traders. The Queen herself was not entirely certain for some time where Hong Kong actually was; the location is said to have been something of a private joke between her and Albert, even when the island itself was named after her). If not for the vision and determination of the "Merchant Princes," Hong Kong might well have been left to languish and eventually die.

Their vision was Hong Kong as an immense entrepôt between China and the rest of the world. The same vision persists even amid today's wealth: With the sudden opening up of China in 1979, Hong Kong's hongs rubbed their hands together in anticipation of an overnight, and even bigger, trading boom. But in the colony's infant days, the traders' hopes were dashed. In the first five years the "rock" just didn't live up to the economic expectations. Immense trade just didn't materialise. And in 1845 the dispirited entrepreneurs actually sent a petition to Whitehall explaining that "such a settlement of Hong Kong was never really required." The colony couldn't

compete with the flourishing Treaty Ports on the Chinese mainland; disease was rife and decimated the early trading community; the Chinese Imperial Court allowed only the poorest, meanest coolies to emigrate to the island, and the bottom began to fall out of the land market.

However, within a matter of three or four years of that letter of dejection, the wheels of commerce finally began to turn. Hong Kong began to generate trade, building gradually from a backwater settlement and pirate haunt to the entrepôt that it was supposed to be. And, having at last got the cash registers tinkling smoothly, the British merchants quickly seized the chance to make their political weight felt. Their next steps established a firm bond between business and bureaucracy, a traditional power-sharing process that has largely ruled Hong Kong — this splendid working example of the corporate state — up until the present day.

The original Hong Kong Charter of 1843 had established essentially the same colonial power structure that exists today — an Executive and a Legislative Council, both appointed by the Governor, and the Governor himself appointed by the Crown and given the power of decree which effectively prevailed over the decisions of his executive and legislative branches. (Interestingly enough, the British at first had no intention of governing the Hong Kong Chinese and considered setting up a separate administration under Chinese law, as they were later to govern African tribes through their own tribal chiefs. But the Chinese preferred British law — punitive as it was in those days — to the Draconian measures of their own Ch'ing dynasty rule and justice).

As for the British merchants, they began clamouring for a share of the political pie. It was they, not the bureaucrats, who had challenged and

Traditional and modern garb mingle in a culturally flexible society.
Over: *In the calculator capital an abacus is often still the more reliable instrument.*

opened up China, and they were not being rewarded enough; and in a campaign not unlike that of Britain's North American colonists, they protested against unfair taxation and demanded some degree of "self-government." In 1850, Whitehall bent to their will and appointed two Unofficial members of the Legislative Council from the business community. In 1857, a third Unofficial took his seat in the policy-making chamber. Thirty years later, the Chamber of Commerce was allowed to nominate its members, and in 1896 even more representatives of the now-dominant merchant ranks were appointed.

From that day to this, government in Hong Kong has been synonymous with a Victorian marriage of business and bureaucracy — Victorian in the sense that in the interplay of passive and dominant roles, the business sector has certainly worn the pants and wielded the rod. True, since the end of the 1960s, in response to pressure from Whitehall and China, *laissez-faire* has been moderated by the government and an enormous programme of social development and welfare undertaken to improve the living conditions and basic quality of life of the working-class Chinese. Massive public housing schemes, improved public health and education, better sports and recreation facilities and a sustained attack on corruption within the civil service have, to a certain extent transformed the colony from a rather disreputable China Coast enclave to something approaching a legitimate, self-examining society. Yet even amid the social and industrial emancipation that exists today, the colony's development continues to be inspired and guided by its traditional dogma — that what's good for the hongs is good for Hong Kong itself.

But that's not to say that the taipans have been entirely autocratic as colonial masters. In one sense, their triumph lies in the fact that while they've managed to dominate the direction and philosophy of Hong Kong's development they've also

maintained their control by gradually giving way to Chinese social and economic pressures. After the colony's birth, it was more than 30 years before a single Chinese was invited to a Government House reception. Even then, there was consternation among the British. But the first of many compromises prevailed. Whereas in India, for example, a native challenge like that was fated to result in a stiffening of British resistance, and disaster, in Hong Kong the taipans simply stiffened their upper lips and muttered all the way to the

European and Chinese — have been able to develop separately, side-by-side, without violent conflict. Culturally, they've always maintained their distance from one another. Politically, they've always agreed that anything but the present status quo could bring the "House of Hong" crashing to the ground — the British view democracy as something that could cause damaging social turmoil in Hong Kong, and the Chinese, having experienced it once in the ill-fated Chinese Republic set up by Sun Yat Sen, are not particularly anxious to try it again.

But the real common ground upon which both societies have met, and will continue to meet, is their mutual love, respect, adoration and pursuit of money. Without money, Hong Kong simply has no reason to exist. In this inter-racial marriage of convenience, British organisation, protection and mercantile strength has been matched with Cantonese diligence and flexibility to create that mighty Asian entrepôt. Since the 1949 revolution in China, there's been a big injection of largely Shanghainese industrial expertise and capital that has turned this island emporium into a major manufacturing centre. And since China'a remarkable change of political direction from revolutionary Maoism to *rapprochement*, modernisation and controlled capitalism, the British have had to loosen and virtually relinquish their grip on the Hong Kong family purse-strings.

But it is a testament to British tenacity, and the triumph of the taipans, that while the balance of power in Hong Kong is no longer synonymous with roast beef and chop suey — in that order — the foreseeable future will simply see it pragmatically reversed, with more chop suey than roast beef.

bank. They soon saw that it was in their best interests to bend to Chinese aspirations, and soon the wealthier, more influencial Chinese were being appointed to the Legislative Council — and drawn into the civil service — where they have been gradually expanding their power ever since.

The result of all this compromise has been Hong Kong's triumph, on the one hand, as an enormous ledger sheet (and, lately, a giant of emerging industrialism in Asia), and as a society in which two distinct and even incomparable races —

Container ships are no competition to the river-travelling junks.

Incense and Industry
The Cultural Heritage

In the shadow of a modern office block, amid the screech and roar of dense urban traffic, a cluster of joss-sticks smoulders and smokes — lighted and placed at the kerbside at dusk to appease capricious spirits.

On a warm balmy night at **Stanley**, the southernmost beachside residential spot on Hong Kong Island, Chinese tom-toms, cymbals and gongs boom and clash and flutes wail as traditional funeral rites begin for a dead village elder — ancient ceremonies that persist alongside luxury expatriate apartment blocks and condominiums that are now being rented for as much as US$7,000 a month.

On the pavements of **Queen's Road East**, one of the main arteries connecting **Central District** with the island's southern beaches, skilled craftsmen tap and chip away at the ornate and intricate carvings that decorate traditional camphorwood chests, working literally within a few feet of cars and buses.

In the early morning sunlight that splashes across the merchant shipping of Victoria Harbour and the towering offices, apartment blocks and hotel complexes of **Causeway Bay**, Chinese men and women gently sway, lunge and pirouette amid the greenery of **Victoria Park**. Their strange ballet is Tai Ch'i, traditional Chinese "shadow-boxing," a form of isometrics and bodily and mental discipline that comes from the softer, philosophical school of *kung-fu*.

Hong Kong's magic and excitement arise from the very extent to which its Chinese heritage has survived, and continues to claim its right to exist, against the shock of urban development. The British claimed the place as a trading post and, for what it was worth, a home away from home for stately colonial

living. But the Chinese have shaped its character with traditions that simply refuse to give way to Western progress — that, and their sheer weight of numbers.

Successive waves of immigration from neighbouring China have swelled their numbers to well over five million and given some of Hong Kong's urban areas — notably **Mongkok** in the hinterland of Kowloon — the dubious distinction of the highest population density in the history of mankind. And density in Hong Kong is gauged by the number of square feet that each person can count on for living space. For Hong Kong's industrial masses, those that scurry and push and shove below the level of wealthy expatriate and Chinese upper-class lifestyles, an apartment is a bunk-bed and the streets provide the only breathing space and room to move between dawn and bed-time. The real shock of Hong Kong's urban jungle is not only its soaring, jampacked skyscrapers and tenements but the teeming street-life that goes on at the roots.

The vast majority of Hong Kong's Chinese come from China's southernmost province, Kwangtung. They're people of the land — rustic, unsophisticated, boisterous, ambitious and certainly among the noisiest people in the world. They've brought their rural heritage with them — with its beliefs, customs and superstitions — and applied it quite successfully to modern industrial life. That's why Hong Kong seems to look and feel like a giant ant's nest that's gone slightly haywire. Aside from the simple battle for living space, their boisterous behaviour and tendency to yell and shriek at each other have made life in the streets an assault upon the nerves and an unashamedly ill-mannered rat-race — yet, in their former rural setting, it was required that normal conversation be conducted loudly and publicly to safeguard against conspiracy and incest within the crowded home; and the only alternative to bad manners in the streets, buses, trams and elevators would probably prove worse. If Hong Kong's Cantonese tried to institute a Japanese-style code of behaviour, with its reticence and bowing and after-you-no-after-you-no-after-you social etiquette, Hong Kong would probably grind to a halt.

But, being rural people, the Cantonese have brought their cultural traditions with

Amid creeping mechanisation these hard working women demonstrate that old manual methods stubbornly survive.

them, and clung to them in the face of Westernised urban development. And it is this surviving culture that has given Hong Kong its distinctive image and its tourist appeal — splashing vivid colour, strange sound, excitement and exotica on to an urban canvas that would otherwise be grey and even forbidding.

The rickshaws are certainly disappearing, but only because there's no room for them any more on the traffic-packed streets, and they're not really part of the Chinese heritage anyway — they were invented by an American in Japan. Otherwise, the stately batwing-sailed junks from Amoy and Swatow still lumber ponderously through the merchant shipping and ferries of Victoria Harbour, whole convoys of these surviving "Big Eyed Chickens," as they're called, hauling cargo from China's factories and communes on the easterly winds.

Coolies still trot through the street-crowds carrying their own cargo, anything from cooked lunches for office-workers to heavy consignments of factory products, slung on both ends of springy split-bamboo poles. *Hakka* women still carry on their traditional work as labourers on building sites, toting rubble and bags of cement and dismantling the fiercely strong yet seemingly flimsy bamboo scaffolding — another tradition in itself — with hardly anything but their eyes showing out of thick swathes of protective clothing, and curtain-like fringes of black material dancing from the rim of their wide rattan hats.

In the more traditional shops and stores, the click and clack of the *abacus*, a simple yet incredibly efficient manual calculator which the Chinese have been using for many centuries, is still competing with the hum of modern digital registers and computers. Pigs are hauled to slaughter in wrought-iron baskets; a truck speeds by with its open load-space packed with live ducks, all huddled together and quacking in the wind — a testament to the way in which

the Chinese, in this age of refrigeration, still don't trust food that's not so fresh that you can still see it twitching.

The herbal medicine shop offers its traditional palliatives and cures of roots and plants, powdered lizards and deer horn, snake bile and fox's bezoar — a few doors down from the modern Western pharmacy, with its drugs and antibiotics. Fortune-tellers divine futures and ward off malicious spirits brave enough to invade the concrete and shrill clamour of the big city blocks. Professional letter-writers and calligraphists work quiety and patiently over their tiny tressle tables at the foot of massive high-rises, their little open-air "offices" looking almost apologetic for the fact that they've somehow managed to command little more than nine square feet of valuable space.

You'll find street-barbers who still specialise in removing women's facial hair with a twisted string, running it back and forth over the cheeks, forehead and upper lip and tweaking it out by the roots. At festival time you'll see them dressing the *long queues*, or pigtails, of the Chinese *amahs* — the traditional housemaids, who have long formed a sort of union or sisterhood in which the rules of membership are celibacy, simple and even severe clothing and hairdos, and a talent for canny business investment. You'll find Hong Kong's Chinese heritage in the raucous clatter and clash of *mah-jong* tiles — by night in the *mah-jong* parlours and tenements, by day in Chinese restaurants along Lockhart Road in Hong Kong Island's **Wanchai** district and in the backstreets of mainland **Tsimshatsui**. You'll find that heritage presented in its most exquisite form in the traditional arts and crafts still being practised amid the plastic, stainless steel and electronics of Space Age Hong Kong — wood, jade and ivory carving, rattan work, porcelain, brass, painting,

---

Enormous bell-shaped incense coils are suspended from the worship hall of the Man Mo Temple.

weaving, embroidery, silver and gold jewellery, even the elementary yet fascinating dexterity of the itinerent craftsmen who fashion grasshoppers out of thin slivers of bamboo (look around the **Star Ferry Concourse** on the Kowloon side) and doll-like stick-figures out of plasticine.

In the middle and late 1960s, Hong Kong was known as the "London of the East" for its red buses, mini-skirts, pop groups and Chelsea-style boutiques. In this era, at the start of the super-technological '80s, the technology is certainly now omnipotent as a cultural force — with an even bigger rash of Chinese discos, Chinese fast-food outlets, Chinese motorcycle clubs, Chinese surf-cats, Chinese beach-barbecues which feature a Chinese passion for powerful Japanese cassette-radios, and a thriving and steadily growing Chinese television, film and advertising industry which is pinning Chinese tastes and aspirations to an encroaching wall of trends dictated by New York and Los Angeles. But the traditional culture somehow continues to hang in there.

Just as the movie and television productions continue to search back among the ancient conflicts and *kung-fu* traditions of Chinese history, the ancient boom, clash and shriek of Cantonese and Pekinese opera can still be heard amid the more modern, synthesized cultural sounds. You'll find both brands of opera — a confusing, garish parade of mythical characters and legends — in the streets at night, in the vast public housing estates, in district cultural centres and distinct townships that have not yet been integrated into the urban sprawl. A daily check of the "Letters" page of the *South China Morning Post* will tell you where to find performances of opera, traditional puppets, traditional ballet, Chinese music recitals and Chinese orchestral concerts.

Alongside the culture, there's the modern-day persistence of Chinese beliefs. And Chinese beliefs are many and complicated. There are about 600 traditional temples in Hong Kong, most of them devoted to ancestor-worship and the Chinese interpretation of the term "religion" in which Buddhism, Taoism, Confucianism and folklore are thrown together with incense, fortune-sticks, calenders, special gods and goddesses to conjure up blessings that are not so much spiritual as worldly and down to earth — health, happiness and luck.

Luck is something that the Chinese have a traditional reverence for — are willing to invest enormous amounts of time, effort and money in the pursuit of. It would be an exaggeration to say that the Chinese would gamble on two flies walking up a wall; by the same token, a social report was issued some years ago that blandly stated that gambling was "not conducive to the basic Chinese character" — and it was greeted with howls of laughter. The passion of the Hong Kong Chinese for gambling is such that this tiny colony boasts one of the biggest and richest, and most religious, horse-racing industries in the world — operated by the Royal Hong Kong Jockey Club at two tracks, **Happy Valley** and **Shatin,** and so powerful that the club itself is a major pillar of the ruling establishment, its profits are so high that it refuses each year to reveal them publicly, and the whole set-up is run on such a relatively big-business scale that it tends to make those of England, America and Australia look like social indulgences by comparison.

If luck is a Holy Grail to the Chinese, health and happiness are so coveted that a 4,000-year-old spiritual science, the geomancy of *fung-shui* (wind and water), is still flourishing today in Hong Kong — its ancient rules, calculations and divinations still consulted when a new home is built, when furniture is being moved around, when a wedding ceremony is being planned or a grave-site is to be established. Essentially, fung-shui places man in the most propitious relationship to his environment, protecting him from malicious or evil influences that would wreck the harmony of his life. The science is not making as

much headway these days in the urban jungle of Hong Kong, where there's little room for harmony anyway, but it's estimated that there are still some 100 professional fung-shui geomancers offering their services around the colony and in recent years they've exorcised a floor of the Internal Revenue Department of evil spirits, established the site of the giant Shaw Bros movie studio at **Clear Water Bay** and even been consulted on the preparations for a land auction staged at the Hilton Hotel.

But the real spiritual passion of the Hong Kong Chinese bursts forth during their traditional feasts and festivals — and without these regular explosions of colour, reverence and sheer excitement, Hong Kong would be just another urban growth-centre, a city without a soul. April, May and June are the best festival months, though at any time of the month, in any month of the year, there's usually some celebration or another going on. Chinese passions really ignite, and the colony's fishing and maritime heritage really emerges, at the annual Tin Hau Festival in May — a time of worship for Tin Hau, the Goddess of the Sea.

Thousands of boat people and urban dwellers who have left the sea for the factories travel to the Tin Hau Temple at **Joss House Bay**, at the eastern gateway to Victoria Harbour — their junks, modern trawlers, launches, ferries and even floating cranes decorated with huge flags and bunting and elaborate altars loaded with offerings to Tin Hau. In April and October there are two festivals in one — Ching Ming, in which the Chinese pay homage to their ancestors by going to the ancestral graves and "spring-cleaning" them, making offerings of food and wine and even, in the case of old-style tombs, taking out the skulls and bones to polish them. One reason for the two separate observances of Ching Ming is that in, crowded Hong Kong, five million people can't all go to the cemeteries and tombs at once; the city would simply seize up.

There are many other festivals in which the Chinese mask is lifted aside to reveal a race of people who really know how, and when, to let their hair down (see

A game of Chinese checkers provides welcome relaxation in a hectic city.

page 64 for full list). Lanterns are lighted and families climb to the tops of hills to gaze upon the moon at the Mid-Autumn or Moon Festival in September. Traditional Dragon Boats burst across the major bays and anchorages in June in races that are a pandemonium of threshing oars and booming drums — an event held to commemorate an ancient hero who drowned himself in protest against government corruption in China.

But there's one festive point of the year when the triumph of the cultural heritage shines through the cloak of commerce and compromise that is the more obvious facade of Hong Kong — and this triumph is a typically and inscrutably Chinese. In May, thousands of people flock to the island of Cheung Chau to take part in the Bun Festival — a four-day mardis gras in which spectacular processions roll along the waterfront and, on the final night, hundreds of young men used to clamber up huge towers of "lucky" buns (the towers are still featured, but the annual scramble has been stopped since one of the pillars collapsed a couple of years ago). This Cheung Chau Festival is not only a local feast, it's also a major tourist drawcard. Each year now, so many tourists turn up that the observance itself is becoming little more than a cultural stage-play for cameras.

But at the same time as the parades and drums and gongs are drawing all those tourists to Cheung Chau, another even more colourful, even more frenetic yet a almost private festival, Tam Kung (Washing of the Buddha), takes place at **Shaukiwan** — the former fishing port at the eastern end of the island side of Victoria Harbour. And here, free of foreigners and the firing squads of camera-shutters, the real uninhibited traditions of the Hong Kong Chinese remain much the same as they have been for many centuries.

Painstakingly applied make-up and elaborate costumes follow hundreds of years of tradition.

33

Island Emporium
The Physical Hong Kong

Hong Kong is made up of nearly 240 islands and a small portion of the south-east tip of mainland China. The entire territory covers a total of 1,055.61 square kilometres with a population of more than five million — around 10 per cent of which is concentrated in two densely crowded urban areas.

The colony is basically divided into four major areas: First is the large island — 75.9 square kilometres — called officially **Hong Kong Island**, but known locally as "The Island." The island is linked to the second most important area, **Kowloon**, by the Star Ferry, the Cross-Harbour Tunnel and the underground Mass Transit Railway. Kowloon is a 10.35 square km peninsula, ranging from the Star Ferry quay to Boundary Street, which marks the start of the **New Territories**. This area in turn comprises 730 square kilometres of once-rural land

stretching to the Chinese border at Lo Wu. The New Territories was leased to Britain in 1898 for 99 years. The fourth major area is the Outlying Islands, mostly stretching to the west in the direction of the small Portuguese enclave of Macau, 60 kilometres away.

The Island

Hong Kong Island is the centre of government, banking and business activity, most of it located, fittingly enough in **Central District.** On the extreme flanks of the island, facing the harbour, are **Western District** and, to the east, **Chai Wan** and **Shaukiwan**. Neither of these districts are visited much by tourists, though both house some of the older and more traditional Chinese communities. Heading into Central from Shaukiwan, the northern side of the

island is an almost continuous belt of industrial, commercial and residential buildings hotels and stores, passing through **Quarry Bay** (mainly warehouses, offices and printing plants), **North Point**, with its ferries to the industrial districts of Kowloon, and then Causeway Bay, tourist and shopping mecca and access point to the Cross-Harbour Tunnel.

CAUSEWAY BAY
Before the tunnel was opened in 1972, Causeway Bay was a fairly uninteresting residential and small business district. Today, it boasts fine shops and huge department stores, three luxury hotels and half a dozen cinemas, as well as restaurants of every Chinese type and foreign nationality. Between Causeway

Bay and Central is the **Wanchai** district — best known for its old "Suzie Wong" bar-girl image and its nearby chrome-and-clip nightclubs. Wanchai now offers good shopping facilities, particularly for electronic goods, along with restaurants and many business locations — and "Suzie Wong" can still be found along Lockhart Road at night.

CENTRAL DISTRICT
Central, or Victoria, as it is officially known, is the business capital of Hong Kong, standing on the island's northern shore facing the mainland across the harbour. It is dominated by the big banks, businesses, shops and three international class hotels. Here, too, are three important ferry piers. Close by the

City Hall cultural complex is the Star Ferry to Kowloon; to the west are the Outlying Ferry Piers to the offshore islands and about a kilometre further west is the Macau Ferry Pier with hydrofoils and ferries to the Portuguese gambling enclave.

WESTERN DISTRICT
After the sophistication of Central, Western offers the tourist a glimpse of old and exotic Hong Kong, with picturesque buildings, steep, narrow streets, workshops where traditional crafts are still practised and some of the older temples. To the extreme west are **West Point** and **Kennedy Town**, once incongruously known as "Chinatown."

VICTORIA PEAK
Crowning Hong Kong island is Victoria Peak (known simply as "The Peak"). A funicular tram to The Peak runs from Central, starting just above the Hilton Hotel. The 400-metre Peak used to be Hong Kong's most exclusive residential area, and here are some of the most extravagent colonial-era houses on the island. There are also interesting walks where one can survey virtually the entire territory, sometimes as far as the Chinese border.

A breath-taking view from Victoria Peak, with the Kowloon peninsula and the New Territories in the background.

MID-LEVELS

A jam-packed high-rise residential belt sandwiched between The Peak and the harbour. The Botanical Gardens are situated here and well worth a visit. To the west, the mid-levels run into the more stately environs of Pokfulam Road, where the University of Hong Kong is located.

THE SOUTH

The southern side of the island is certainly the prettiest and has some of the best beaches in Hong Kong. To the east of the southern coastline are **Big Wave Bay** and **Shek O Beach** and toward the west, **Tai Tam Bay**. Next to Tai Tam is a series of bays and coves, each with their village communities and offering fairly good recreational facilities: **Repulse Bay**, **Deep Water Bay** and the fishing villages of **Stanley and Aberdeen**. Between Deep Water Bay and Aberdeen is the splendid all-purpose "oceanarium," **Ocean Park**, with a magnificent aquarium, ornamental gardens, the world's biggest cable car ropeway and the largest ocean theatre in the world, too.

A general word of warning: From May to the Mid-Autumn festival in October, nearly all beaches are terribly overcrowded and are to be avoided, especially on Sundays.

The Mainland: Kowloon

TSIMSHATSUI

Unfortunately, most tourists see only the tip of Kowloon, Tsimshatsui, which has the shops, hotels and bars. The easiest and most convenient shopping is next to the Star Ferry in Star House, Ocean Terminal and Ocean Centre. Small, exclusive boutiques selling imported goods line Nathan Road, the main thoroughfare heading north, and the many streets leading off it.

North-west of Tsimshatsui is **Yaumatei**, with its typhoon shelter and the Jordan Road ferry. Yaumatei leads to Mongkok, one of the most densely populated areas in the territory.

To the east of Tsimshatsui is **Kai Tak** international airport, and to the north are **Boundary Street** and the **New Territories**.

On the outlying islands and in the New Territories precious agricultural land is tended by age-old methods.

NEW TERRITORIES
Some of the New Territories, which stretch up to the Chinese border, is still unspoiled, but the last decade has seen extensive industrial and residential development in the "New Towns," **Shatin, Tsuen Wan** and **Tuen Mun**, part of a huge population resettlement programme to ease "people pressure" on the urban areas. Outside the urban areas, the New Territories features old walled villages, rural architecture, farming and most remarkable countryside. The most picturesque area is the **Sai Kung Peninsula** which juts out to the right of Kowloon. To the east lies **Tolo Harbour** and to the west, Tai Mo Shan, the highest mountain in Hong Kong, and **Castle Peak**. Other towns on the tourist route are **Tai Po, Fanling**, with its excellent golf course, and **Sheung Shui**, the last stop before the border town of Lo Wu.

THE ISLANDS
Of Hong Kong's 238 islands, few are inhabited and even fewer visited. **Lantau** is the largest (more than twice the size of Hong Kong island, at 141.96 square kilometres) with a population of a mere 20,000. Lantau has good walks and some interesting Buddhist temples and Christian monasteries.

Cheung Chau
Originally a notorious pirate haunt, today it has a large expatriate community and many of the locals speak English. Cheung Chau's main industry is based on boat-building and allied crafts. The harbour is packed with hundreds of junks and sampans and there are many little artisan workshops throughout the island.

Peng Chau
Situated just off Lantau, Peng Chau is a quiet little backwater community about a square kilometre in area with a population of 8,000 who fish, farm and work in light industry. There are no cars and you can walk round the island in less than an hour.

Lamma and Po Toi
Until recently the most unspoilt of the major islands, now the construction of a power station on the north side of the island has disrupted its tranquil atmosphere. There are ferry stops at the two main villages of Yung Shue Wan and Sok Kwu Wan, and there's a pleasant two-hour walk linking them. But it's still popular with campers and has some excellent restaurants specialising in seafood. **Po Toi**: Hong Kong's southern-most island, is particularly famous for its 3,500 year-old carvings on Ghost Rock, thought to be Khmer, Burmese or Indian in origin. The island has several deserted villages, with all but about 200 of the locals having left to seek their fortune in Hong Kong or beyond.

Ping Chau
A tiny island just off the coast of China. During the past 20 years its population has dwindled to about 20 and abandoned huts on the island can be rented for about $3 a night. Nearby lies **Kat O**, the most remote of the inhabited islands. The ferry journey, like the one to Ping Chau, is lovely, taking the visitor through Tolo Harbour to the farthest reaches of the New Territories.

The South China Sea provides a living to those who are able to abide by its rhythm.

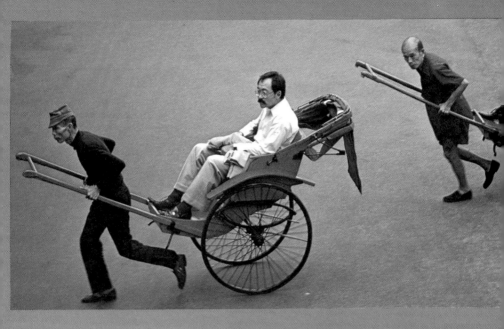

The Tourist Trail
On The Beaten Track

"On a dank winter's day shortly after the Chinese New Year, the population of Upper Lascar Row in Hong Kong was enjoying its mid-morning snack of beche-de-mer and jasmine tea when the street was galvanised by the advent of a quarter of foreign devils so manifestly aching to be plundered that a mighty hosanna welled up the length of Queen's Road, Central. Abacuses began clicking furiously, catchpenny ivories of the goddess Kwan Yin bloomed on every curio dealer's shelf, factory-fresh Ming horses were hastily baptised with dust to simulate age, and tempting whiffs of Lapsang Soochong wafted about to decoy the Outer Barbarian."

S.J. Perelman, **Swiss Family Perelman.**

Shopping

Although Hong Kong has far more to offer than just shopping, to the tourist Hong Kong is synonomous with bargains. It has something for everyone, with any budget — from the large department stores selling luxury imported goods to the colourful street hawkers with their fake "Gucci" handbags.

The main shopping districts on the island are Central and Causeway Bay. The *Bargain Guide To Shopping In Hong Kong*, published by the Hong Kong Tourist Association, is indispensible for any shopper. This excellent guide gives all names, addresses, telephone numbers and map locations of all shops listed and, more important, also gives recommended prices.

If you're looking for antiques, the late Mr Perelman notwithstanding, a visit to Hollywood Road and Upper Lascar Row (Cat Street) in Central is a definite must.

If you are a collector or want to be one, then Luen Chai at 22 Upper Lascar Row should be on your shopping agenda. Specialising in antique ceramics, Luen

Chai has one of Hong Kong's most comprehensive stocks of porcelains from the Ch'ing dynasty.

Though many of the porcelain items are extremely expensive simply because they are genuinely of great value, they are augmented by less expensive items such as bamboo brush pots, snuff bottles, jade carvings, cloisonne and scrolls. In **Hollywood Road** is another store worth a visit, **Yue Po Chai** curios, opposite the **Man Mo** temple — the oldest in Hong Kong. Yue Po Chai houses a variety of oriental antiques ranging from porcelain, ivory carvings, jade jewellery, wood carvings, screens, paintings, embroidery to furniture. Other antique and ivory stores can be found in **Wellington Street** and along **Lyndhurst Terrace**.

Moving west along Hollywood Road you'll see that both sides of street are lined with arts and curio shops. You'll also find ivory factories here and Chinese herbalists with their bizarre array of prophylactic fungi and antelope horn tonics. There are many stalls in this area which specialise in making *chops* — ivory and porcelain seals used as name stamps. Give them your name and for about $50 they'll make you a chop

bearing the characters of its Chinese translation. A reputable chop shop is **Tsui Man Hin** in **Man Wah Lane** in **Bonham Strand East**. For a good Chinese herbalist try **Eu Yan Sang** at 109-115 **Queen's Road, Central**.

Also on Queen's Road, opposite the market, you'll find the **Chinese Merchandise Emporium** which is the oldest of a number of department stores selling products of the People's Republic of China, from clothing to foodstuffs, jewellery to bicycles to household goods and antiques. Walking back along Queen's Road in the direction of Star Ferry you'll find two Western-style department stores. **Wing On**, which is owned by a Hong Kong Chinese family, and the British **Lane Crawford** selling imported clothing, cosmetics and household goods. The newly opened **Landmark** shopping centre, above the Des Voeux Road exit of Chater MTR Station is a visual and shopping delight.

Continue east to Wanchai. Hennessy Road, which has, among other shopping attractions, many furniture worshops specialising in rattan ware, runs into the island's next big shopping centre, **Causeway Bay**. Here, are many shops specialising in cameras, electronic goods and clothing. Lane Crawford has another branch here and there are two huge Japanese-owned department stores, **Daimaru** and **Matsuzakaya** which again sell imported goods, obviously from Japan.

Opposite **Victoria Park** stands the **China Products Store**, which, like the Chinese Emporium, sells just about every art and craft and consumer item produced in the People's Republic. It is the largest of the entire chain in Hong Kong, and features the same icy air-conditioning in summer.

Aside from the stores, a wander through the streets and alleys of Hong Kong will introduce you to the "street

people." like the sidewalk barbers, professional letter writers for people who can't read or write, and hawkers peddling everything from fruit to locally made denim jeans.

Shopping in Kowloon

The main shopping areas are situated in **Tsimshatsui** at the **Ocean Centre, Ocean Terminal** and **Star House, New World Shopping Centre** and along **Nathan Road**. The first three, on the Star Ferry concourse, are enormous shopping complexes selling every kind of merchandise and for forth is making a spirited bid to rival the first three in size and variety. Here, you can find antiques and curios, leather goods, shoes, clothing, cameras and every kind of electronic

The patient collector is bound to be satisfied in shops like this — abounding around Hollywood Road.

gadget; and there are several reasonable bookshops. **Nathan Road** features expensive boutiques selling French and Italian fashions, several department stores — **Shui Hing** and **Lane Crawford** — and more branches of **China Products**. Nathan Road is also a centre for tailors who can run up silk shirts and suits in as little as twenty-four hours. However, if is bargains you're looking for it's best to get away from the main shopping areas and into the side streets. Ivory and jade factories can be found in **Granville Road** and **Kimberly Road**. If it's jade you're after try the **Canton Road** jade market, though unless you are an expert it really is advisable to take someone with you who knows what to look for.

Kowloon City Market is the place for locally manufactured clothing — anything from suits to socks. Real bargains, such as cashmere sweaters, can be found but you need to be discerning.

Bargaining: Don't buy things until you've checked the prices at least at half a dozen other places. Shopkeepers expect this so don't be put off by black looks — it's all part of the game. They also expect to be asked for their "very best prices." Exceptions to this are the large department stores and exclusive shops where prices are fixed and usually clearly marked. Also, it is not worth while haggling over items that cost only a few cents in street markets.

Warning: whatever your bargaining prowess, don't let your ambitions get in the way of quality, especially with artwork, electronic goods and cameras.

Shopping Tips: Check with consulates or trade missions for the latest custom requirements before agreeing to goods being mailed or shipped home. Insist on insurance coverage for goods to be mailed or shipped to ensure safe arrival. Ignore touts and don't patronise a shopkeeper who beckons you or tries to grab at you from his doorway. Ensure that sample material is obtained if suits or dresses are to be custom-made. Ensure that model numbers of watches, cameras,

tape recorders etc, are noted in invoices or receipts to avoid misunderstanding and always insist on the manufacturer's guarantee. Not all shops accept credit cards, so establish that you intend to use one before bargaining and buying. Those that do accept credit cards demand a five per cent to six per cent "tax" — so watch what that does to your "bargain price."

Be careful when buying ivory — it could be fake. Genuine elephant tusk ivory has a cross-hatch pattern on flat surfaces which distinguishes it from plastic. Be warned, also, that some countries will now not allow "new" ivory to be imported.

Before buying diamonds visit the Diamond Information Centre at 22 Wyndham Street, Central, (tel: 5-251191) for information and lists of accredited shops.

Shopping Hours: There are no fixed shopping hours, but generally it's Hong Kong Island, Central District 9 a.m. — 6 p.m., Causeway Bay and Kowloon Commercial District 10 a.m. to 10 p.m.

Hong Kong's shopping centres mushroom, permitting to trade airconditioned comfort against originality.

Transport

There are numerous ways of getting round Hong Kong, and public transport is efficient, despite continual traffic jams. Naturally, it is wise to avoid rush hours.

TRAMS

Hong Kong's unique double-decker trams run the full length of Hong Kong Island from Kennedy Town in the west to Shaukiwan at the eastern tip. All for a flat fare of 30¢! It's a good way of seeing the street-life of Hong Kong, and the whole journey takes about two hours. You can also hire trams for private tours or parties.

BUSES

The two bus companies operate throughout the colony. Fares range from 50¢ to $3. The China Motor Bus fleet has a cream and blue livery at that of

Kowloon Motor Bus Cream and Red. Each company operates through the harbour tunnel. All routes are point to point and buses return on the same routing. The main town terminuses are situated near **Star Ferry**, **Central District**, **Admiralty MTR Station** on Hong Kong Island and **Star Ferry**, **Jordan Road Ferry** in **Kowloon**.

TAXIS

These operate only in Hong Kong, Kowloon and the New Territories. In Hong Kong and Kowloon taxis are red and silver grey. Here the flag-fall is $4.00 and 50¢ for each subsequent one fifth kilometre. The fare through the Cross Harbour Tunnel costs an extra $10. New Territories taxis have a green body and white roof. The flag-fall is $2.40 and 40¢ for each subsequent one fifth kilometre. It's not unknown for drivers to overcharge tourists. If that happens take down the licence number and report it to

PEAK TRAM
If you are going to The Peak then the funicular Peak Tram is the easiest and most exciting way. Sensational views across the rooftops to the harbour for a $2 single fare.

STAR FERRY
The Star Ferry runs every five minutes and takes about seven minutes to cross the harbour between Central and Tsimshatsui. It costs 50¢ to travel on the upper deck, 30¢ for the lower. There are also other cross harbour ferries, and a vehicular service which takes longer.
The Star Ferry operates from 6. a.m. to 1 a.m. but if you get caught on the wrong side of the harbour in the early hours you can take a small boat, known as a **wallah wallah**. These run between Kowloon Public Pier and Queen's Pier on Hong Kong island. $13 per boat or $2.00 per person.

RICKSHAWS
A few elderly rickshaw runners still operate on both sides of the Star Ferry concourse, mainly for the benefit of tourists. The fare is approximately $5 for every five minutes or a few hundred metres. Be sure to settle the price and destination before boarding, or rather clambering, in.

MASS TRANSIT RAILWAY
The first stage of Hong Kong's underground railway opened in October 1979; the cross-harbour link to Central four months later. The total journey time between Chater Station in Central and Kwun Tong in Kowloon is less than 30 minutes, including stops at each station. Fares range from $1.20 to $3.20. The next stage, a $4,000 million extension to Tsuen Wan new town will be opened by the end of 1982, by which time it's estimated the MTR will carry 1.8 million passengers each day.

the police. Taxis are notoriously hard to find at rush hours and impossible when it's raining. Do not take "Pak Pai" or unmarked taxis without meters, and don't expect people to queue — you'll need your elbows and a lot of swift footwork to compete for cabs outside the ranks. Also, don't be surprised if the above fares have risen again, perhaps doubled, by the time you visit the colony.

MINI-BUSES
These yellow and red vehicles are the next popular form of transport after buses. They ply the roads on both sides of the harbour and stop anywhere except bus stops and restricted areas. Fares range from $1 to $3. Those crossing the harbour usually charge a minimum of $3. Maxi-cabs — yellow with a green stripe — are like mini-buses. They run from The Peak to Central and from Aberdeen to Central and Causeway Bay. The fare is $2.

Public transport makes use of Hong Kong's natural environment — sea and mountains.

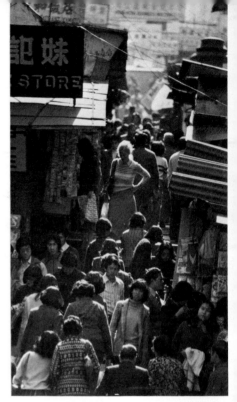

RAILWAY

The Kowloon-Canton railway runs about twenty departures each day from Hung Hom station in Kowloon to Lo Wu on the Chinese border. A through-service to Guangzhou (Canton) was started in 1979 and the line is presently being adapted for electrification. At Lo Wu passengers for Guangzhou (Canton) must leave the train and walk 300 metres across the border to the Chinese National Railways station at Shum Chun. Visitors to Hong Kong are only allowed as far as Sheung Shui, the station before Lo Wu. The entire journey takes about 40 minutes. The fares are $4.20 for first class and $2.10 ordinary class. Additional services are run on Sundays and public holidays but as the trains are packed to capacity it's best to avoid them. The Hong Kong trains have no toilets aboard them too.

CAR HIRE

There are a number of care hire companies for self-drive or chauffeur-driven rental. Self-drive usually includes unlimited mileage but not petrol. Daily rates vary from $100 to $200 depending on the company and the car. Anyone over 18 years of age with a valid overseas licence can legally drive in Hong Kong.

Sightseeing

Tucked away behind Hong Kong's high-rise concrete jungle a myriad pleasures await the tourist.

CENTRAL

Starting in **Central**, as you come off Star Ferry — to the left is the City Hall complex with its concert halls, theatre and Museum of Art, which contains Chinese art and antiquities, including paintings, calligraphy, rubbings, ceramics, bronzes, lacquer-ware and jade. There are also a number of fine and interesting paintings and prints from old Hong Kong. The museum is on the 10th and 11th floors and is open daily, except Thursday. Afternoons only on Sundays and public holidays. Admission free. Opposite City Hall is the white painted and Victorian-looking **Hong Kong Club**, looking a little down-at-heel now and due for demolition some day. Across Chater Road is the Supreme Court building which fronts on to Chater Square. Opposite the square are the three brooding financial monoliths, the Bank of China, the Hong Kong and Shanghai Bank and the Chartered Bank. Moving from Central into **Western** district, follow Queen's Road to Hillier Street, turn left

and climb the steps into Upper Lascar Row, also known as Cat Street, with its antique and bric-a-brac stalls. Walk up from Cat Street to the **Man Mo Temple**. One of the oldest temples in Hong Kong, it is dedicated to the god of civil servants and a famous second century warrior. Inside are sedan chairs used to carry the gods at festival time, and two engraved bells, the larger one dated 1847.

The area around Man Mo Temple was used as the location for the shooting of the film *The World of Suzie Wong*, though much of it is being redeveloped now.

A flight of steps next to the temple leads to Ladder Street and its colourful clothing and haberdashery stalls. After exploring Ladder Street, continue left along Hollywood Road, noted for its arts and antique shops, undertakers and coffin makers, and into **Possession Street**.

Up — the only way to go in a crowded city.

This is where the Union Jack was first raised when the British landed at Hong Kong on January 26, 1841.

Walk from Hollywood Road into Garden Road until you reach the **Botanical Gardens**. This little oasis was established more than 100 years ago and has some 300 species of birds and hundreds of exotic trees, plants and shrubs. The gardens are opposite **Government House**, the official residence of the governor. The residence is not open to the public, except for once a year, in the springtime, when the prized azaleas are in magnificent bloom in the grounds and thousands make a pilgrimage to view them.

On **Garden Road** is the **Peak Tram** terminus. The tram opened in 1888 and has never recorded an accident. The $2 single fare takes you to the **Peak Tower** complex with its restaurants and breathtaking views. Victoria Peak has always been "the" place to live since the British entered Hong Kong. Until the Japanese occupation in the Second World War, Chinese were forbidden to have homes there. You can walk round The Peak in less than an hour, taking in the whole panoramic circle of Hong Kong from the Sai Kung Peninsula to Aberdeen, over the islands of Cheung Chau, Lamma and Lantau, and, on a clear day, even Macau.

WANCHAI

Now you've explored Central and The Peak, move on to **Wanchai**, the old "red light" district, with its many surviving topless bars, massage parlours and tattooists. This district is now being extensively redeveloped, though, and much of its charm and character is giving way to Central's high-rise commercial and residential overspill. Suzie Wong herself has trimmed her long hair, changed into denim jeans and found greater fulfillment in the factories.

Wanchai has many good restaurants but a noval way of dining out is to eat at the many open-air stalls which line the side-streets. Proceed along **Hennessy**

Road to **Causeway Bay**. If you wish, you can make a slight detour to the original and most historic of Hong Kong's two racecourses, at Happy Valley.

CAUSEWAY BAY

Although Causeway Bay is predominately a business, shopping and residential area, it does have a few places of interest to the tourist.

On the waterfront is the **Typhoon Shelter**, with its floating population, both Chinese and foreign, living on junks and sampans. Next door is the headquarters of the **Royal Hong Kong Yacht Club**, and the district's best known landmark, the **Noon-day Gun**, of Noel Coward's *Mad Dogs and Englishmen* fame. It stands in a small garden opposite the **Excelsior Hotel** and is still fired daily. Opposite the typhoon shelter is **Victoria Park**, which has a large swimming pool, tennis and squash courts and football pitches, as well as leafy walks which make the bustle of Hong Kong seem a long way away. But not the noise.

Behind the park in **Tin Hau Temple Road** is a shrine dedicated to **Tin Hau**, goddess of the sea. In the opposite direction **Tai Hang Road** leads to **Tiger Balm Gardens**, an eccentric landmark with its pagoda and grottoes, stone sculptures and gaudily painted reliefs depicting events in Chinese mythology. A jade collection is housed in a reproduction Chinese mansion. The gardens have a frankly garish charm and are a good place to take children, but, again, are earmarked for demolition and redevelopment into something more in keeping with Hong Kong's future.

To the east, **North Point** and **Shaukiwan** have little to offer the tourist except some ship's chandlers and the **Tam Kung** temple dedicated to a local child-god in Shaukiwan. In May, there's a fantastic festival here that very few tourists know about.

The cold facade of concrete sky — scrapers hides soft skin and sweet song.

SOUTH ISLAND BEACHES

Once out of the built-up areas, you'll find some of Hong Kong's most picturesque countryside and its most popular beaches. Take a No. 14 bus from Shaukiwan to **Stanley village**. It's a scenic trip along **Tai Tam Road** to the reservoir, then along **Tai Tam Bay** to Stanley. This former fishing village has long been a popular and fashionable home for expatriates. The British Army is based at Stanley Fort, so English is spoken in most shops. There is an excellent street-market which is a popular but a crowded and claustrophobic shopping centre for inexpensive but good-quality denims and other clothing. The main street, fronting the main beach, boasts an English-style pub. This beach, is small but "ungazetted" and not highly recommended for swimming. For water sports, take a No. 9 bus from Shaukiwan to **Shek O** and **Big Wave Bay** beaches. Both have changing rooms, toilet facilities, lifeguards and a flag system to warn if the sea is too rough.

Hong Kong's most popular beach is at **Repulse Bay**, but that means that from May to October it is packed with bathers, especially at weekends. If you prefer something a little more dignified than trying to laze around on a square foot of sand on the beach, the **Repulse Bay Hotel** offers nostalgia and a taste of old colonial elegance. Sip a drink on the terrace or beneath the old Maugham-era overhead fans and look out on the human sardines around the bay.

Next stop on the coast is **Deep Water Bay** and **Ocean Park**. The park is built on two levels, Lowland and Highland complexes, connected by an exciting cable car ride. At the entrance are landscaped gardens, a small zoo for the children, an aviary and a marine theatre where penguins and sea-lions perform. Here, you can also watch Chinese opera and a parrot that rides a bike on a circus wire.

Take the cable car to the Highland area of the oceanarium where there is a much bigger marine theatre with dolphins, seals and a killer whale; also, the fascinating Atoll Reef, a giant three-level aquarium housing a man-made pool and a coral island teeming with

everything from tiny coloured tropical fish to sharks.

Wave Cove is a specially constructed stretch of shore-line with a mechanically produced "surf" where sea-lions, walruses and penguins play in the waves. Best to visit during the week, as it is extremely crowded at weekends.

ABERDEEN

Aberdeen is the home of Hong Kong's biggest fishing fleet, and 65,000 people live on the 3,000 or so junks which pack the harbour. Apart from the harbour life and the huge floating restaurants, which serve sea-food at exorbitant prices,

Aberdeen also features a vast, jam-packed floating community of boat-people awaiting resettlement on shore.

HONG KONG UNIVERSITY

You can take the road from Aberdeen to Central. The University, in **Pokfulam**, has a museum of bronzes from the Tang, Shang, Chou and Yuan dynasties, Han Tomb pottery and ceramics from the Ming, Ch'ing, Tang and Sung periods.

POOR MAN'S NIGHTCLUB

Full circle and back in Central. Coming from the west of the island, and just before the Star Ferry you find the Macau Ferry Pier. By day a car park, but at night it is transformed with dozens of little stalls selling cassettes, clothes, souvenirs and trinkets. There are also food stalls specialising in seafood; plates of steaming clams, mussels and Chinese beer and a chance to watch the world go by. Be careful about buying cassettes, though. Chances are that they're "pirate" tapes, badly recorded and likely to prove a disappointment when you put them on your own player.

Dolphins keep well away from fishing fleets and villages — but they can be seen in Ocean Peak.

Kowloon Sightseeing

Kowloon, (literally "Nine Dragons", after the range of nine hills which look down upon it) is situated on the Chinese mainland. This isn't at all obvious in **Tsimshatsui** near the Star Ferry, but becomes more so as you move out toward the New Territories. So why not try something different? Instead of taking the Star Ferry from Hong Kong to Kowloon, take the one to **Jordan Road**, where the Western influence hasn't yet really established itself.

JADE MARKET

Right by the ferry, on **Canton Road**, is the **Jade Market**. To the Chinese, jade means everything: Prosperity, wealth, perfection, authority and good health too. A drink of finely-ground fresh jade traditionally relieved asthma and kept one's hair glossy.

Every morning between 10.00 a.m. and midday the jade stalls line the street. But be *very* careful. Jade dealers are often ready to put fakes in with the genuine goods and it's best to take along either a Chinese friend or someone who knows what to watch for. Experts say the only real test of jade is to scratch it with a knife to see if it marks, but few people care to take the risk! Opinions vary on which is the best jade to buy. Some say the whiter and clearer the better, others swear by bright green and then there are those who say buy it only when it is turning brown as this indicates age.

Street markets abound — there is nothing one cannot buy — and often it is prepared on the spot.

TEMPLE STREET

Walk down **Canton Road** or **Shanghai Street** to Temple Street. During the day time, Temple Street, named after the Tin Hau temple, is a riot of food stalls and hawkers, but at night it is a colourful carnival, showing old Hong Kong at its best. On Sundays, there are usually Chinese opera performances on the street. Crowds, pavements heaped high with T-shirts, transistor radios, old clocks, new calculators, an assortment of hi-fi equipment at very low prices, used books, blue jeans, Mickey Mouse watches, and playing card kings — all this is Temple Street.

MONGKOK

At first glance, Mongkok may not seem to have much to offer, aside from its obvious reputation as one of the most crowded places in the world. But it is worth more than the casual visit. For here are the snake shops (snake is a traditional Chinese winter food), tea wholesalers, antique dealers and stores specialising in traditional Chinese clothing. Of particular interest is the **Koon Nam Wah** company in Shanghai Street, which specialises in Chinese wedding gowns. Nearby, in **Sai Yeung Choi Street** is the snake specialist **She Wong Yuen**. The shop offers snake meat, snake liver for medicinal purposes and snake wine. And, if you want to try such delicacies as snake soup or fried snake, She Wong Yuen has a restaurant too in **Tung Choi Street**.

LEI CHENG UK MUSEUM

This museum is built on the site of a Han tomb, discovered in 1955. The tomb, dating from between 25 and 220 AD, is made of bricks. There are four chambers in the shape of a cross and a central chamber with a domed vault. A number of funerary objects found inside are on display. There are also specimens of typical pottery and cooking and eating utensils from Han times. The tomb and museum are in **Tonkin Street** on the **Lei Cheng Uk resettlement estate** in **Shamshuipo**. Both are open daily from midday until 7 p.m., except Tuesdays. Admission 10¢.

LAICHIKOK AMUSEMENT PARK

In addition to the usual fairground dodgems, swings and slot machines, this amusement park has a small zoo, a copy of a famous Canton lake, a Ch'ing dynasty garden and a replica Sung dynasty village with a herbalist shop, curio shops, an art gallery, a magistrates court and a monkey stall all in the "main street." There is a village tea house serving Cantonese *dim sum*. The village is built round an artificial lake on which you can take a ride in a sampan. You can also tour the village by sedan chair, which you pick up in the main street.

The art gallery shows reproductions of Sung art and a calligrapher demonstrates the technique of Chinese writing. In the evenings there is Chinese opera. But be warned: The admission fee is high-$70 for adults for the full Sung dynasty tour.

KOWLOON WALLED CITY

Of little historic or cultural value. The walls date back to the last century, when this small area of Kowloon was retained by China after Hong Kong was relinquished to the British. Today, it is largely a ghetto inhabited mainly by many drug addicts. If you are curious enough to go there, the Walled City runs along **Carpenter Road**, up **Lung Kong Road** from **Prince Edward Road**. Don't go in groups of more than two or three, don't be nose and it's advisable not to take cameras.

PENINSULA HOTEL

If you're tired after a shopping or sightseeing expedition, the famous high-ceilinged lobby of the **Peninsula Hotel** in **Salisbury Road** is a pleasant place to relax over a cup of tea or a drink. This is Hong Kong's most prestigious watering hole so you'll have to pay over the odds. But it's fun to sit and try to pick out the celebrities who stay here. The rules are rather snobby here, though. If you're

wearing "rucksack" gear or open sandals, the waiters will invariously refuse to serve you. The Peninsula has a commercial *penchant* for up-market tourists and the "beautiful people."

New Territories and Outlying Islands

The New Territories stretch from Kowloon peninsula to the Chinese border. Apart from the three satellite towns of **Shatin, Tsuen Wan** and **Tuen Mun**, the area is relatively unspoilt. This is the more traditional Hong Kong, the Hong Kong of rice paddies, old walled villages, fishermen, misty mountains and monasteries.

Transport is easy. Taxis are cheap, buses and mini-buses run regularly from one spot to another. The train goes to the border.

SHATIN
Shatin's **Temple of 10,000 Buddhas** really does have more than 10,000 — the inner walls are lined with them. There are other temples in the grounds containing huge gold-leafed statues and the bizarre "human Buddha," the strangely preserved body of the founding abbot, Yuet Kai. Yuet Kai was 87 when he died in 1965. He had been a strict vegetarian for nearly 70 years and wrote nearly 100 books on Buddhism. In accordance with his instructions, his body was placed in a sitting position in a square box and buried in the hillside behind the temples which he himself had built. After eight months the body was exhumed. Eyewitnesses say there was hardly any sign of decay and that the body had a phosphorescent glow. It was then covered in gold leaf and robed, and now sits in state in a glass case in the temple of **Man Fat**.

Shatin Pagoda: Yuet Kai was also responsible for the construction of the nine-storey pagoda in the temple grounds.

Squatterhuts are slowly replaced by more adequate housing.

CHINESE UNIVERSITY

Nearby is a Catholic monastery where pottery depicting the life of Christ in Chinese characters is on sale. The Chinese University is actually a series of different colleges once founded by missionary groups, but now totally secular. Here, you should visit the museum with its modern paintings and collection of 300 ancient bronze seals.

AMAH ROCK

The "amah" or housemaid, stands with her back to **Shatin**. Legend has it that a fisherman's wife, with her baby strapped to her back always went to the spot to watch for her husband's return. When he perished on a trip, the gods took pity on her and with a lightning bolt, transported her and the child to join her husband in heaven, leaving a natural stone monument to her fierce loyalty.

SHATIN RACECOURSE

The impressive Shatin racecourse, the most modern in Asia, was opened in October 1978 at a cost of $550 million. Built entirely on reclaimed land, the huge complex has a completely computerised totalisator, which is one of the most advanced in the world. Absolutely packed with punters on major race days, and well worth avoiding if you prefer a "Sandown" atmosphere.

SAI KUNG PENINSULA

Jutting out to the east of Kowloon, the peninsula has some of the best beaches in the territory. It's rugged coastline and hills make the area ideal for hiking, camping, fishing and sailing. There are many good walks. The town of Sai Kung is an interesting little place. Some good seafood restaurants, a little market square with an old temple.

TIN HAU TEMPLE

This temple in **Joss House Bay** is one of the oldest of those dedicated to Tin Hau, Queen of Heaven and guardian of all those connected with the sea. A temple was first built on this site in 1226. For

most of the year it is seldom visited, but in May when this Taoist deity's birthday is celebrated, about 30 thousand people come to the temple to pay homage and thousands more just to look. Marvellously decorated boats, lion dances and elaborate rites turn this festival into one of the most colourful and explosive in Hong Kong. Special ferries are put on for the occasion, and though they are crowded, it is worth the effort to see how the Chinese really let their hair down.

However, "off-season" times and not Tin Hau festival are advised for browsing around the temple, which is a satisfying experience. On the main altar, two statues of Tin Hau sit side-by-side. The

goddess is guarded by two female attendants and two legendary generals said to have the power to hear or see anything over any distance. In the main palace are two two-metre replicas of junks, complete with sailors and guns. At festival time offerings are laid out on their decks.

TAI PO
One train stop beyond Shatin is **Tai Po Kau** and here a ferry boat leaves each day for trips around **Tolo Harbour**. Visit **Tai Mei Tuk**, a village near the **Plover Cove** reservoir and you'll get an impression of the colossal amount of work that was needed to turn what was a sea-inlet into a vast man-made reservoir.

Buses leave Tai Po, this pleasant market town, for **Kadoorie Farm**, established in the early 1950's to give refugees from China a chance to learn modern agriculture. Tai Po town also has the famous **Tai Ping** carpet mills, where you can purchase the goods virtually at cost.

FANLING
The **Royal Hong Kong Golf Club** has its main links at Fanling. Renowned as one of the best in the region, it is said to be the founding course and doyen of the Asian Circuit. The Jockey Club's riding and country club is also based at Fanling.

Further on is **Sheung Shui**, a few miles from which the Chinese border can be viewed from the **Lok Ma Chau** lookout. With a telescope it is possible to see life in the Chinese village on the other side of the Shum Chun river, which is the international boundary. Moving west to **Yuen Long**, another rapidly expanding market town, you find the 400-year-old walled village at **Kam Tin**, two miles on, complete with moat and walls. The village is a rare example of ancient community life outside China. All the residents are members of the worldwide Tang clan.

Small boats, wooden vats and salted fish still find a market.

Outlying Islands

LANTAU

The largest island, it has several places of interest. The **Po Lin** Monastery, 800 metres above sea level, serves inexpensive food in its large dining room and has a student hostel, also very cheap, for overnight accomodation. Ferries for Lantau leave from the outlying ferry pier in Central, near the **Macau Ferry terminus**. There are two services, one to **Silvermine Bay**, on the east of Lantau island, the other to the village of **Tai O** on the west.

Lantau has some good beaches and some of the best country walks in Hong Kong, along with a Trappist monastery and even a small but still-flourishing tea plantation.

CHEUNG CHAU

Seven kilometres east of Hong Kong, off the southern tip of Lantau. Plenty to see. You can walk around the entire island in less than two hours. Charming winding side streets, markets, food stalls, a harbour and fishermen, as well as the **Pak Tai Temple** and the famous pirate haunt, **Cheung Po Chai** cave. Also the site of the frenetic annual Bun Festival.

LAMMA AND PO TOI

The most unspoilt of the islands: Archeologists are discovering continuing evidence that Lamma was the home of Stone Age man. Good walks and several fine seafood restaurants. **Po Toi**: Only a few hundred people live here now. Many deserted houses are testimony that the population has dispersed to seek their fortunes either in Hong Kong or further afield. Interesting carvings on **Ghost Rock**, thought to be 3,500 years old. Also the location of the best, and most uninhibited Tin Hau celebrations in May each year.

Festivals

When it comes to festivals and holidays, Hong Kong people have the best of both

Eastern and Western events. They live both according to the Western calendar with the major Christian festivals, and the Lunar calendar which marks Chinese feast days and celebrations thousands of years old.

Almost every month brings forth different festivals, but, because most are dictated by the Lunar year (the position of the moon) it is difficult to ascertain exactly when each will take place. Here, though, is a selection:

JANUARY

New Year's Day, of course. One of several "New Year's" (Chinese, Indian, Jewish, Buddhist) celebrated by different communities. New Year's Eve is celebrated as everywhere else, with parties, walks, crowds gathering in Central to splash around in the fountains in Edinburgh Place.

FEBRUARY

Chinese New Year. This can take place any time from the last week in January almost to March. To foreigners, it is one of the fascinating holidays, though everything around town seems to be closed. Basically for the Chinese family, with children given money, with cleaning of houses, with flowers, and with everybody wishing each other "Kung Hei

All year long traditional festivals keep the incense burning.

Fat Choy." In the traditional Chinese districts there are lion and dragon dances, and a lot of feasting. Victoria Park becomes a blaze of New Year flowers and traditional tiny orange trees with little fruits.

Hong Kong Arts Festival Barely a decade old, but during February, the Urban Council brings in different orchestras, choruses, soloists and dramatic groups from all over the Oriental and Western worlds for two weeks of the arts. Most of the performances are at City Hall. This festival is strictly for the culturally minded, but some traditional Chinese and Asian attractions are interesting to the casual visitor.

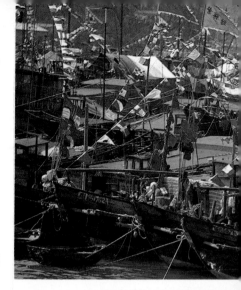

APRIL

Ching Ming Festival This is the time for Chinese to visit the graves of their ancestors at the cemeteries, to sweep and clean the graves, light incense and pay homage. It is also, unfortunately, the time for forest fires, since picnics are usually held after the sweeping of the graves, which are often in wooded areas.

Easter. An official holiday, though few Chinese are Christians. Good Friday is also a public holiday. It's more a convenient escape-value for tensions in the huge industrial dormitories of Kowloon and its urban hinterlands.

MAY

Tin Hau Festival. Hong Kong may seem industrialised — but its maritime beginnings are recalled in this, the birthday of the most important goddess of all: the Heavenly Queen, the Goddess of fishermen. All fishing craft are marvellously decorated and fisherfolk gather at temples in **Joss House Bay**, **Yaumatei**, **Stanley** and **Deep Water Bay** to pay homage to her. The most important and impressive celebration is at Joss House Bay, with lion dances and rites. Special ferries are put on for the occasion. And though they are crowded to the point of bursting, it's worth the extra effort to see this colourful

celebration. **Poi Toi** has the best traditional celebration, but you would have to charter a boat to get there.

Tam Kung Festival. This May festival is staged to commemorate the birth of Buddha and is celebrated in **Shaukiwan** at the **Tam Kung Temple.**

Birthday of Lord Buddha. Religious celebrations in Buddhist temples. At **Lantau** and **Shaukiwan**, the Buddha statues are bathed, and many devotees journey out to **Po Lin Monastery** for the affair.

Cheung Chau Festival (Bun Festival). Four days of celebration at **Cheung Chau Island**, where the great symbol is buns. The buns symbolise good luck, and until a few years ago, huge 60-foot bun towers were erected, with the people scrambling up to get the highest one. Alas, an accident prompted the government to curtail this part of the celebration. But there are still the colourful dances, operas, processions (especially on the third day), and flower arches. Interestingly enough, this is one festival when great feasts aren't so important. Traditionally, only vegetarian food is served: No pig or chicken is killed on land, and the fishing junks lie at their moorings without casting a net. The only exception is that oysters are allowed to be eaten. Definitely worth a trip out to see the fun.

JUNE

Dragon Boat Festival (Tuen Ng). This festival commemorates the death of a national hero who killed himself by drowning in protest against a corrupt government. It is said that a kind of dumpling was thrown into the river to feed the fish which would otherwise have eaten his body, and the water was beaten with paddles to scare off other fish. The dumplings are still made today (and eaten with relish), while the paddles are used on special boats with the head and tail of a

Children delight in showing off their brilliantly coloured costumes during festival times.

dragon, racing with each other. Lots of noise, drums, competitions everywhere in the colony where there's water. The most traditional races take place at **Stanley** and in the New Territories. But now Dragon Boat Racing has become big tourist business, so the international races are run off in **Yaumati** and **Repulse Bay**. Newspapers carry full reports on the best places to view this exciting cultural sport.

JULY

Birthday of Lu Pan. Mid-July, the birthday of the Chinese Master Builder is celebrated. Architects and builders hold dinners, but the most important celebrations are at **Lu Pan Temple** in **Kennedy Town** on the island.

AUGUST

Maiden's Festival. Also known as the Seven Sisters Festival, it's held on the seventh day of the seventh moon. It's essentially a celebration for girls and young lovers and has its origin in Chinese folklore dating back more than 1,500 years.

Festival of the Hungry Ghosts. Usually held in August, it celebrates the night when ghosts roam the world, having been released from purgatory. In some areas of Hong Kong, small roadside fires can be seen where paper money, fruits, and other offerings are burnt to appease them.

SEPTEMBER

Mid-Autumn or Lantern Festival. One of the most important festivals. Special mooncakes are eaten (recalling a 14th Century revolt against the Mongols when the secret plans for revolution was hidden inside the cakes). Special lanterns are lighted, and children stay up late to see the moon rise. Naturally, the best places are the highest, like The Peak and mountains in **Lantau**. Later the mooncakes are eaten. The **Lantern Festival** in **Victoria Park** is heavily patronised — and everybody carries lanterns to celebrate the occasion. An all-night festival which is great fun, just for the experience of a colourful and

reverend Chinese observance.

OCTOBER

Birthday of Confucius. The beginning of October was the birthday of Confucius. Not much to do, but if you wish, go to the **Confucius Temple** in **Causeway Bay** on Caroline Road to watch the celebrants.

Chung Yeung Festival. Like the Ching Ming Festival, this is the time for families to visit their cemeteries and pay homage to their ancestors. Another part of the festival is to climb to a high peak to avoid disaster. This comes from an old story about a man advised to get away from the city to avoid a major catastrophe. When he came back he found that all living things had perished suddenly during his absence.

Festival of Asian Arts. October 1980 was the fifth Annual Festival of Asian Arts, sponsored by the Urban Council. The two-week celebration is the only one in Asia bringing together musical, dramatic and artistic events, recitals, lectures and exhibitions from at lease a dozen countries in the region. A superb event which, unfortunately, has not had enough publicity abroad. Programmes are available through the **Urban Council, City Hall High Block**, Hong Kong.

chefs.

Hong Kong cuisine is hardly limited to the Chinese. A profusion of excellent Japanese, Korean, Thai, Vietnamese, Malay, Indian, Ceylonese and Indonesian restaurants are scattered all though the colony; and hotels vie with each other in offering superb French and Swiss cuisine. In the New Territories, a little restaurant lists 65 different curries on its menu — curries from as far north as Afghanistan, as far south as Ceylon and Sumatra.

Food

Once upon a time, a Hungarian cook by the name of Vladimir Sis decided to write poetry about Chinese food, and one of the poems went as follows:

"I had a dream
In which I watched as the court jewellers
Offered all their most precious gems of every
colour
For the same number of opaque grains of rice."

Mr. Sis wasn't much of a poet — but he did interpret the spirit of Hong Kong. For if Mammon and money rules 99 percent of Hong Kong, the one percent which gains the most respect is the Chinese cuisine. The top restaurants and clubs spend fortunes on hiring (and stealing from each other) the best Chinese

Chinese Food

Chinese food is classified according to region of origin, the major types are:

CANTONESE (Southern)
Certainly the most predominant — and the most variety and highest quality. Virtually every block has its Cantonese restaurants, which can range from noodle shops to full-scale restaurants with 500 different dishes. Poultry, pork, beef and seafood are the popular ingredients, with an endless variety of mushrooms and fungi. The emphasis isn't on great sauces, but the natural tastes and colours,

---

Joss-sticks, flowers and lanterns all help to express reverence or joy.

through "stir-frying," on those huge saucepans called **woks**, and steaming. Some specialities here would be **Won Ton Soup, fried noodles, crystal shrimp or chicken**, and the usual sweet and sour things . . . but mind you, somebody once said that there were 25,000 different Cantonese recipes, so a few days in Hong Kong won't exactly give a complete taste of this great cuisine.

PEKINESE (Northern)
Most visitors like to try **Peking Duck** while here, and they're in luck with the plethora of Pekinese restaurants. The force-fed and "inflated" duck is basted with a special sauce prepared from soya beans, sugar and other condiments and roasted to a dark rich brown; it is then served in three courses. First the skin is dipped in thick soya bean paste with raw green onions wrapped in Chinese pancakes, next the meat is served in a similar manner, lastly the bones of the duck are boiled into soup with cabbage and mushrooms.

Other specialities of Peking include **Mongolian hot pot**, excellent fish, enormous white cabbages and, during the wintertime, fine barbecued lamb and mutton. The Pekinese rarely use rice and are fond of wheat dumplings and noodles.

SHANGHAINESE (Central)
Next in popularity are Shanghai dishes. Actually, Shanghai doesn't have that much of an indigenous cuisine. It takes its ingredients from the sea, and its recipes from the classical cities around it. Shanghai food itself is rather oily for some tastes, but nobody can ever resist its **braised eel** (usually double-fried), its ham in a honey sauce, or its **squirrel fish** — so called because it actually "chatters" when the sauce is poured atop it.

SZECHUAN (Central)
If you **really** like your food spicy, then try one of the Szechuan restaurants, with their hot, sour, sweet and salty dishes. **Szechuan shrimp with garlic sauce** is a

tasty favourite, as is smoked **Szechuan duck**.
Note: Chinese food is not ordinarily ordered individually as is Western food — instead, the dishes are ordered and shared by all. For this reason the more people in your party, the more variety in your meal. If there are just two of you, order one main dish, plus a soup and fried rice (**Chow Fan**).

DIM SUM
Chances are that you'll want to visit a Chinese teahouse around breakfast or noontime. Good — this is the time to savour "dim sum", which literally means "little hearts." These are Chinese hors d'oeuvres, which are steamed, baked, fried little cakes of fish, pork, beef and vegetables, sometimes with bits of dough or noodles. In a way, dim sum is the easiest way to choose Chinese food: When you see a tray coming along, simply point to what you want. The bill is added up by counting the number of baskets on your table. Most dim sum restaurants serve between 10 and 15 different dim sum daily, but the famous may have up to 40 around lunchtime.

Mouth-watering Chinese food is available in never-ending varieties, though roast pig is usually reserved for celebration dinners.

Restaurants

FOOD STREET

Food Street in **Causeway Bay** isn't to
everyone's liking, but it is still a spectacle.
On two pedestrian streets, totalling
8,000 square metres are 28 of the most
diverse eating places. Employing 600
waiters and 200 chefs, with menus listing
more than 2,000 dishes, more than
100,000 people gorge themselves weekly
on Peking Duck, Punjab dahl, Cantonese
dim sum, Hangchow Beggar's Chicken
and Australian steak, etc., etc.

LOK YU TEA HOUSE

24-26 Stanley Street, Central 5-246029
(Cantonese). Noted as much for
traditional atmosphere as for its fine
food. Ceiling fans, blackwood tables, high
backed chairs with built-in mirrors, brass
spittoons. Marvellous **dim sum** dishes at
lunchtime including meat dumplings with
orange peel, pastries stuffed with mashed
chestnuts and sticky rice steamed in lotus
leaves. From the English menu,
barbecued pork loin ($18) is a good
starter and sliced duck with ginger is
recommended. Other dishes worth trying:
Bamboo shoots with shrimps ($30), fried
frogs legs with oyster sauce ($46), and
steamed minced pork with salted duck
eggs ($16).

LYCHEE VILLAGE

17-19 Wellington Street, Central 5-
245688 and 9-11a Cameron Road,
Kowloon 3-686544. (Cantonese) Famous
for its casseroles and soups, particularly
sharksfin and crabmeat ($18 per person).
Other specialities are pan-sauteed duck in
lemon sauce ($60), soyed pigeon ($38),
and shredded cuttle fish with bean
sprouts ($30). Good desserts.

HOOVER SKY

66 Yee Wo Street, Causeway Bay 5-
770339 (Peking). Said to serve the best
Peking food in town. The speciality here
is Peking barbecued duck ($80), though
chicken a la Hoover ($90) roasted with a
rich stuffing of pork and vegetables is

also recommended, as are chicken in paper ($30) and shrimps on toast ($28).

SZE CHUEN LAU
466 Lockhart Road, Wanchai 5-7902571 (Szechuan). Consistently high standard. Smoked duck ($90), and steamed Szechuen pork with vegetables ($65), and braised stone fish (seasonal price) all highly praised. Chili prawns (seasonal price) and eggplant in garlic ($16) also good.

AU TROU NORMAND
6 Hankow Road, Kowloon 3-668754 (French). Classic French cooking. Good fish dishes : Bouillabaisse Marseillaise is served every Friday ($56). Wan Yiu citronelle ($48) freshwater fish in lemon sauce recommended. Good patés and cheese.

LANDAU'S
257 Gloucester Road, Causeway Bay, 5-7902901 (English) Daily roasts are a feature. Traditional dishes such as steak and kidney pudding and treacle pudding praised by nostalgic British visitors. Good range of hors d'oeuvres, pickled herrings ($15), escargôts a la Bordelaise ($20.00, 1/2 doz) and homemade goose liver terrine ($18). Expensive, but thoroughly enjoyable.

Hong Kong's many first-class hotels offer sumptuous daily lunch buffets which leave nobody hungry.

INTERNATIONAL

Beefeater
Basement, Shui Hing Building, 23
Nathan Road, Kowloon; English.
3-671893

Bauhinia Room
6/F., The Hongkong Hotel Kowloon;
Chinese/European.
3-676011

Brewery
3/F., Ocean Centre, Kowloon; European.
3-690603

Cafe d'Amigo
79A Wong Nai Chung Road Hong
Kong; French.
5-772202, 5-778993

Chesa
1/F., The Peninsula, Kowloon; Swiss.
3-666251

Gaddi's
G/F., The Peninsula, Kowloon; French.
3-666251

Gaylord
43 Chatham Road, Kowloon; Indian.
3-675039

Godown Restaurant
Basement, Sutherland House, Chater
Road, Hong Kong; European.
3-221608

Grandstand
4/F., Sheraton Hotel Kowloon; Grill.
3-691111

Hugo's
2/F., Hyatt Regency Hotel Kowloon;
European.
3-662321

Imperial
1/F., Imperial Hotel Kowloon;
European.
3-662201

Jimmy's Kitchen
Hotung House, Hankow Road Kowloon,
and South China Building Wyndham
Street, Central District Hong Kong;
European.
3-684027, 5-265293

Juno Revolving Restaurant
26/F., 655 Nathan Road, Kowloon;
European/Chinese.
3-960101

La Taverna
Hong Kong Central (Off Wyndham
Street), and 36-38 AshleyRoad Kowloon;
5-228904, 5-772426, 3-691945

Lindy's
57 Peking Road, Kowloon and
Wyndham Street/Queen's Road Hong
Kong; American.
3-671683, 5-222271

Ned Kelly's
11A Ashley Road Kowloon; Australian.
3-660562

Noon Gun
3/F., World Trade Centre Causeway
Bay, Hong Kong; Grill.
5-767365

Paprika
1/F.,Ocean Centre Kowloon; Hungarian.
3-690806

Peak Tower
The Peak, Hong Kong;
European/Chinese.
5-97260, 5-97262

---

*The best cuisine and the best view can be
savoured in one day.*

Pink Giraffe
Top Floor Sheraton Hotel Kowloon;
International.
3-691111

Spaghetti House
3-B Cameron Road Kowloon; Italian.
3-688635

Spicemarket
1/F., Ocean Terminal Kowloon; S.E.
Asian.
3-676238

Stoned Crow
12 Middle Avenue Kowloon; Australian.
3-668494

Tai Pan Grill
6/F., The Hongkong Hotel Kowloon;
Grill.
3-676011

Verandah
1/F., The Peninsula Kowloon;
Continental.
3-666251

Viking
Grand Hotel Kowloon; International.
3-669331

JAPANESE

Izutsu
14/F., Metropolitan Bank Bldg. 25
Carnarvon Road, Kowloon; Japanese.
3-682121, 3-697371

Kanetanaka
Hotel Plaza, 28/F., Hong Kong;
Japanese.
5-7905424

CHINESE

Aberdeen Floating Restaurant
Shum Wan, Wong Chuk Hang Hong
Kong; Cantonese.
5-539111

Ambassador Restaurant
363-373 Nathan Road, Kowloon;
Cantonese.
3-301233

Boil & Boil Wonderful Restaurant
Food Street, Causeway Bay, Hong Kong;
Cantonese.
5-779788

Chinese Palace Restaurant
36-34 Nathan Road, Kowloon;
Cantonese.
3-680343

Chinese Restaurant
Sheraton Hotel Nathan Road, Kowloon;
Cantonese.
3-687131

Diamond Restaurant
265-275 Des Voeux Road C. Hong
Kong; and 90 Queen's Road Central
Hong Kong; and 483 Lockhart Road
Hong Kong; Cantonese.
5-444921, 5-231282, 5-765403

Dim Sum Kitchen
Food Street, Causeway Bay Hong Kong;
Cantonese.
5-777286

Flying Dragon Restaurant
79 Waterloo Road Kowloon; Cantonese.
3-025111

Forum Restaurant
479 Lockhart Road, Causeway Bay,
Hong Kong; Cantonese.
5-778386, 5-778387

Gay Villa
Tai Wai, Shatin; Cantonese.
12-620880

Golden Crown Restaurant
66-70 Nathan Road Kowloon;
Cantonese.
3-666291

Golden Glory Restaurant
16 Carnarvon Road Kowloon;
Cantonese.
3-676586

Golden Capital Restaurant
Chung King Mansion 36 Nathan Road
Kowloon; Cantonese.
3-681844

Highball Restaurant
2/F., Manson House 74 Nathan Road
Kowloon; Cantonese.
3-679021

Hing Sheung Fung Restaurant
86 Waterloo Road, Kowloon; Cantonese.
3-300261

Jade Garden Restaurant
Harbour Village, Star House, Kowloon;
and Tun Ying Building 100 Nathan
Road, Kowloon; and Hyde Park
Mansion 53 Paterson Street, Hong Kong;
and Connaught Centre Central District,
Hong Kong; Cantonese.
3-661326, 3-674041
3-778282, 5-238811

Kam Cheuk Seafood
18 Hanoi Road, Kowloon; Cantonese.
3-668477

Kingsland Restaurant
Hotel Miramar Arcade, Kowloon;
Cantonese.
3-677061

Koon Sang Yuen
32-34 Lock Road, Kowloon; Cantonese.
3-689005

Kowloon Sun Tung Lok
39 Mody Road, Kowloon; and 86
Waterloo Road, Kowloon; Cantonese.
3-670806, 3-045111

Sun Tung Lok Shark's Fin Restaurant
78 Morrison Hill Road, Hong Kong; and
16-18 Penington Road Hong Kong;
Cantonese.
5-748261, 5-762020

Lo Fung Restaurant
The Peak, Hong Kong; Cantonese.
5-96688

Luk Yu Teahouse
26 Stanley Street, Hong Kong; Cantonese.
5-235464

Lung Wah Hotel
Lot 156, Ha Wo Che Shatin, New
Territories; Cantonese.
12-611829

Lychee Village Restaurant
G/F., 15D-19 Wellington Street; Hong
Kong; and Basement, 9-11 Cameron
Road, Kowloon; Cantonese.
5-245688, 3-686544

May Flower Restaurant
6 Tonnochy Road, Hong Kong;
Cantonese.
5-724311

Metropole Restaurant
436-8 King's Road, Hong Kong;
Cantonese.
5-630221

Ocean Palace Restaurant
4/F., Ocean Centre, Kowloon;
Cantonese.
3-677111

Oceania Restaurant
281 Ocean Terminal, Kowloon;
Cantonese.
3-670181

Pearl City Restaurant
Pearl City Mansion 36 Paterson Street,
Hong Kong; Cantonese.
5-778226

Phoenix Restaurant
Food Street Causeway Bay, Hong Kong;
Cantonese.
5-777973

*Floating seafood restaurants in Aberdeen
transport customers by* sampan.

Ping Shan Restaurant
Lido Complex Beach Road, Repulse Bay
Hong Kong; Cantonese.
5-921557

Regent's Sea Food & Shark's Fin Restaurant
17 Heung Sze Wui Street, Tai Po Market
New Territories; Cantonese.
12-668248

Riverside Restaurant
Food Street Causeway Bay, Hong Kong;
Cantonese.
5-779733

Sea Palace Floating Restaurant
Shum Wan, Wong Chuk Hang, Hong
Kong; Cantonese.
5-527340

Shatin Floating Restaurant
Shatin, New Territories; Cantonese.
12-613221

Siu Lam Kung Seafood Restaurant
22 Hanoi Road, Kowloon; Cantonese.
3-667957

Sky King Restaurant
655 Nathan Road, Kowloon; Cantonese.
3-960952

Snake King Restaurant & Barbecue Paradise
6 Fuk Tsun Street Kowloon; Cantonese.
3-925079

Tai Pak Seafood Restaurant
Shum Wan, Wong Chuk Hang, Hong
Kong; and 19 Miles, Castle Peak Bay
New Territories; Cantonese.
5-525953, 12-816451

Ying King Restaurant
179 Johnston Road Wanchai, Hong
Kong; Cantonese.
5-720311

Yucca de Lac Restaurant
Ma Liu Shui, Shatin, New Territories;
Cantonese.
12-612011

Yung Kee Restaurant
36-40 Wellington Street Hong Kong;
Cantonese.
5-232343

New American Restaurant
177-9 Wanchai Road, Hong Kong;
Pekingnese.
5-750458

North China Restaurant
7 Hart Avenue, Kowloon; Pekingnese.
3-668239

Peking Garden Restaurant
Excelsior Hotel, Hong Kong; and Swire
House, 1/F., Hong Kong; and 1 Hysan
Avenue, Hong Kong; Pekingnese.
5-777231, 5-239966, 5-779332

Peking Restaurant
1/F., 227 Nathan Road, Kowloon;
Pekingnese.
3-671315

Peking Restaurant
144 Gloucester Road, Hong Kong;
Pekingnese.
5-754212

Pleasure Restaurant
45-47 Carnarvon Road, Kowloon;
Pekingnese.
3-660408

Princess Garden Restaurant
1/F., Miramar Hotel Building, Kowloon;
Pekingnese.
3-691234

Spring Deer Restaurant
1/F., 42 Mody Road, Kowloon;
Pekingnese.
3-664012

Tien Heung Lau Restaurant
18C Austin Avenue, Kowloon;
Pekingnese.
3-689660

Great Shanghai Restaurant
26 Prat Avenue, Kowloon; Shanghainese.
3-668158

Shanghai Four Five Six Restaurant
340-342 King's Road, Hong Kong;
Shanghainese.
5-700863

Shanghai Lao Cheng Hsing Restaurant
9 Stanley Street, Hong Kong;
Shanghainese.
5-245099

Cleveland Szechuen Restaurant
Food Street Causeway Bay, Hong Kong;
Szechuen.
5-763876

Hong Kong Fung Lum Restaurant
20-22 Leighton Road   Hong Kong;
Szechuen.
5-773235

Red Pepper Restaurant
7 Lan Fong Road, Causeway Bay, Hong
Kong; Szechuen.
5-768046

Szechuen Lau Restaurant
466 Lockhart Road, Hong Kong;
Szechuen.
5-7902571

VEGETARIAN

Choi Kun Heung
G/F., 219E Nathan Road, Kowloon;
Vegetarian.
3-667185

Nuts Ltd.
17-19 On Lan Street, Hong Kong;
Vegetarian.
5-247437

Wishful Cottage
336 Lockhart Road Lok Yau Building
Hong Kong; Vegetarian.
5-734194

*Just like in the old days dried goods are
available in many shops — although fresh
food can be obtained all year round now.*

Sports

Hong Kong is probably the most sports-minded territory in Asia, outside of sports-crazy Japan. Just about every sport is catered for here. But one warning, which is very strict: **Don't** ever imagine that you'll be able to play golf or squash or tennis on the weekends. These are chaotic times at best, miserable at worst, and usually a combination of the two. Weekdays, when the locals are working, is the time for tourists to enjoy the best of Hong Kong sports.

ALL SPORTS

One organisation, the **South China Athletic Association**, caters for almost everything. Annual membership is $40, but visitors need only pay $20 for a month at the Association. The club office at **Caroline Hill Stadium** can answer all questions. Telephone them at 5-776932. They have excellent facilities for track and field events, bowling, table tennis, judo, gymnastics, swimming, squash, badminton, basketball and a health club. And they can make arrangements for yoga, karate, go-karting, hunting and fishing. On Kowloon side, they have a tennis court in King's Park. And there's a driving range for golfers.

CRICKET

The **Hong Kong Cricket Club** is the place to learn about matches. Telephone 5-746266.

BOWLING

Hong Kong has nearly a dozen bowling alleys, with costs up to $8.00 a game. All can be found in the yellow pages of the phone directory.

GOLF

The best course in Hong Kong is undoubtedly the **Royal Hong Kong Golf Club** in Fanling in the New Territories. Three spacious courses, and superb facilities, laid out over 400 acres of luxurious valley. Visitors can play Mondays through Fridays, with green fees around $300 per day. Hotels can usually make arrangements. Otherwise, telephone 12-901211/5. Another course is operated at **Deep Water Bay**, with weekday facilities for visitors. For members of overseas golf clubs, Fanling has very cheap boarding facilities.

Two favourite English sports remain high in course — especially horse-racing attracts tens of thousands of Hong Kong people every week-end.

MOUNTAINEERING
A half-dozen mountains are worth climbing here. Information can be obtained from **Mountaineer and Traveller Service Co.** Telephone 3-801154. If no English is spoken, ask HKTA to help or call **Mountaineering Club**, 5-742391.

SKIN-DIVING
Equipment, information, boats etc. can be obtained from **Sea Dragon Skin Diving Club**, 167 Sai Yee Street, Kowloon. Telephone 3-951942.

SQUASH AND TENNIS
There are many private clubs around Hong Kong. The South China Athletic Association has good facilities. On Hong Kong side. The 17-court Hong Kong Tennis Centre in Wong Nei Chong Gap Road is your best bet, though the courts are often heavily booked.

ICE-SKATING
Ice-skating??? Well, if you're so inclined, then travel to **Laichikok Amusement Park**, where an 18,000 square metre rink can fit 350 skaters. Charges are $18 for two hours, including the hiring of skating boots. Foreigners are a novelty and can easily make friends here. The rink is open from 11.00 am-10.30 pm weekdays, and 10.00 am-10.30 pm weekends and holidays.

SAILING
It isn't easy to find crews just like that — but if interested in trying, or a member of an overseas club, then call the **Royal Hong Kong Yacht Club** at 5-769822. Or try and wangle an invitation to lunch or drinks at the club, which is in the typhoon anchorage opposite the **World Trade Centre**, Causeway Bay.

SWIMMING
During summer weekends at any of Hong Kong's 40 gazetted beaches, bodies are crammed against one another

heartlessly. Other times, the beaches are excellent, kept in good shape by the Urban Council. The most popular is Repulse Bay Beach on Hong Kong side. For the islands, try Lantau's beaches. Shek-O and Big Wave Bay are relatively emptier. Easy to make friends here.

WATER-SKIING
The **Deep Water Bay Speed Boat Company** has equipment and boats, for around $120 an hour. For information, telephone 5-920391 or 5-693177.

BODY-BUILDING
Your best bet is the **Chinese YMCA** (telephone 3-880111) or the South China Athletic Association.

TAI CHI CHUAN
This is the famed Chinese art of toning up the muscles, almost like shadow-boxing, and very, very graceful. There's no law against trying it, if you rise early enough.

Places to see it at its best are the **Botanical Gardens** and **Victoria Park** on Hong Kong side.

HORSE-RACING
The season is from October to May, on Saturday afternoons and Wednesday nights. The two courses are **Happy Valley** and **Shatin**, and tourists can gain admission to the Members' Enclosure by applying to the HKTA, 35th floor, Connaught Centre, along with their passport and $40.

RIDING
There are a number of equestrian schools in Hong Kong, but most insist that one ride under tuition. One exception is in a verdant section of Hong Kong Island, the **Pokfulam Riding School** at 75 Bonham Road (Telephone 5-501359). Open every day from 8.00 am-6.00 pm, their main business is in giving lessons, but with a days' notice, they will rent out horses for $80 an hour. In New Territories, the **Shatin Riding School** hires horses at around $50 per half hour. They're open Sundays but closed on Mondays. Telephone them at 12-611410.

CYCLING
Unpopular, and certainly **not** recommended on Hong Kong's heavily conjested roads. However, bicycles can be hired at Silvermine Bay on Lantau Island which has little traffic.

You can also hire bikes at Shek O on Hong Kong Island, but not advisable at crowded weekends.

For the more esoteric sports, HKTA can supply information. Otherwise, try the Sports Desk of either the **South China Morning Post** (5-620161) or **Hong Kong Standard** (5-616222).

Early morning risers will enjoy watching tai chi chuan *in all parks — or may be even participate.*

Passport to Adventure
Off The Tourist Track

If you still have time left after the shopping and sight-seeing. Hong Kong still has much to offer in the way of unusual things to see and do along the by-ways off the tourist trail.

Visit a Junkyard

Not your usual junk, but a Chinese junk — one of the hardiest vessels on the sea. While motorised launches and new-style trawlers are quickly becoming a way of life, **Aberdeen** and **Aplichau** on the southern side of Hong Kong island, are famous for junk-building. You'll find the **Sau Kee** shipyard on Aplichau constructing, as it has done for the last 30 years, vessels ranging from seven metre pleasure junks to 30 metre ocean-going giants. Although electric drills have replaced heated iron rods, little has changed in this traditional craft — the workmen at Sau Kee still use no blueprints and rely on innate skill and intuition to shape the awkward high-sterned vessels. Another traditional craftmanship can be watched at **Hop Loi's workshop** in Chengtu Road on the Aberdeen side. Here, coopers turn out wooden fish barrels. Again, production techniques are almost as ancient as the Chinese fishing industry itself. After touring the boatyard, why not hire a sampan for half an hour (don't pay more than $25). Go right into the harbour and the "floating township" and marvel at life in the floating metropolis.

Traditional Crafts

Other practitioners of traditional crafts can be found at the **Harbour Village** on the 4th floor of **Star House** near the Tsimshatsui Star Ferry. Here are some of the finest artisans displaying calligraphy, Chinese brush painting, wood and jade carving, fortune telling, paper cutting, flour doll making and many more. The same crafts are performed on Hong Kong side in **Yee Tung Village** on the second floor of the **Excelsior Hotel shopping** arcade.Both exhibitions are free, but all the goods are for sale. Harbour Village is open between 10.00 a.m. and 7 p.m. and Yee Tung Village between 10.30 a.m. and 10 p.m.

The side-streets of Kowloon are a veritable mine of attractions. Herbalists, snake shops and paper shops that sell all manner of paper items — houses, cars, rickshaws and even aeroplanes which are burnt at funerals to ensure that the departing spirit enjoys all the comforts he or she knew on earth — plus a few luxuries they could never have afforded. Paper banknotes, made out to the "Bank of Hell," are also consigned to the funeral fires. During the Mid-Autumn festival these shops sell pretty paper lanterns in a variety of shapes: Butterflies for longevity, lobsters for happiness.

You can visit an ivory factory, like **Oriental Ivory Arts** at **16 Granville Road, 9th floor.** There you'll see craftsmen producing the exquisiting carved artwork that's on sale in the tourist shops of Nathan Road and Tsimshatsui. It's an art handed down from one family generation to another.

For Bird Fanciers

Another exotic place is an old Chinese tea house in Mongkok, called **Wan Loy restaurant**, located at the corner of **Shanghai** and **Soya Streets**. Here, the speciality of the house is fighting birds — finches, thrushes and warblers that are trained to peck and jab and flutter at each other in a bid to force each other back from the open doors of their cages. Though it sounds cruel, the fights are, in fact, the normal thrust-and-retreat territorial rituals of nature, and the birds

rarely hurt each other.

Aside from bird fighting, the restaurant is also a haven for pure bird fanciers — men who pay hundreds of dollars for beautiful species to just show them off in ornate cages, hear them sing and take them for walks in the parks in the cool of the evening.

A few discreet inquiries at the Wan Loy Restaurant will lead you to stalls which sell crickets (the grasshopper variety) which are also prized for their beauty and music — some older generation Chinese carry them in intricately woven rattan pouches on their belts. There are also cricket fighting contests, and dog fights, but the latter are strictly illegal, as is the eating of dog itself.

For other bird lovers there are sanctuaries at **Sha Tau Kok** and on the **Mai Po** marshes and **Lo Wu** near the border, but special permission may have to be obtained because of security in these areas. Walking in the New Territories is a marvellous experience which should not be missed if you have time to roam the countryside.

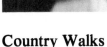

Country Walks

Here are two suggested walks: The first for the experienced or energetic, the second for those who prefer a more leisurely pace. **Sai Kung to Ma On Shan,** 13 kilometres, five hours.

Take a No. 92 or No. 293 bus to Sai Kung from **Choi Hung**. Alight at the terminus in Sai Kung. From the terminus turn right and walk up the road for about a kilometre until you reach the village of **Sha Kok Mei** on the left. Walk through the village keeping the stream in view to the right until you reach the dam. Cross the dam and walk up the road. Continue until you reach a track through the woods on your right. Follow the track as it meanders through the woods until you reach a clearing on your left containing two small huts. Cross the clearing and take the path going up in the centre of the cleared tree-line.

Continue through the trees until you come out into the open. Walk upwards until the path joins the top of the ridge. On the right are several peaks, this is **Ma On Shan** and is a favourite challenge for rock-climbers. Once on top of the ridge turn right and follow the path over the little peak and eventually to the summit. Looking straight across the Tolo Harbour there is Plover Cove, on the left Shatin and on the right **Three Fathom Cove**. Return to Sai Kung by retracing the path.

Eagles Nest Nature Trail. Four kilometres, 1-1/2 hours. Take a No. 71 bus from **Jordan Road**, get off at **Shek Li Pui reservoir**. Walk along the road until you reach the turn-off to the right. Take this road as far as the trail which bears left just prior to the fire control centre. Proceed along the trail (following the posts) through pleasant woodland until, one and a half kilometres later, the signposts indicate a set of steps. Climb up for a fine view of the surrounding countryside and industrial Kowloon in the distance. On this walk you'll spot monkeys in the trees and there's plenty of interesting birds and fauna.

Old arts such as calligraphy and carving can be observed in the Harbour and Yee Tung Villages, right in the heart of town.

Continue round the Eagles Nest and back to the starting point.

Sun Yat Sen's Farmhouse

Situated on the southern side of the bay at **Tuen Mun**, this rather nondescript farmhouse once gave sancturary at various times to Dr. Sun Yat Sen, founder of the Chinese Republic, during his fight from exile at the turn of the century to overthrow China's Manchu rulers. Today, the "Old Red House," as it's called, has been brightened up and together with a statue and memorial obelisk stands watch over **Tuen Mun New Town.**

Overnight on Lantau

Recently, a group of Australian Navy personnel camped out on Lantau rather than haunt the bars of Wanchai. The islands are becoming more and more popular with visitors and Lantau offers two interesting places to stay.

The **Po Lin** or **Precious Lotus Monastery** is well known for its vegetarian food but you can also stay overnight here. There are two dormitories; sexes are segregated at $35 per person per night. The price includes three meals.

You can also spend the night on Hong Kong's only tea plantation on **Lantau**

cubic metres of water. Its surface extends for about 5.6 kilometres with the level six metres above sea-level and the entire expanse covering an area of 690 hectares. It far outranks Hong Kong's first seabed reservoir Plover Cove which has a capacity of 230 cubic metres. Both are worth visiting if only to marvel at the colossal feat of engineering needed for such huge projects. Permission to inspect both dams can be obtained from the Public Works Department or through the HKTA.

New Towns

The development of the three "New Towns" **Shatin**, **Tuen Mun** and **Tsuen Wan** began in 1972. The US$2,000 million development project has enabled the Hong Kong Government to transform what were originally three small market towns into cities capable of absorbing 1.5 million people within ten years. Not the most exciting places in the territory but a massive exercise in town planning and a sophisticated variation of that old university exercise of packing as many students as possible into a public telephone booth.

Peak. Chalet accomodation here ranges from $100 for a chalet sleeping four people to $15 per person for the dormitory chalet. There is a restaurant serving western and Chinese food and you can also taste the locally grown teas. Necessary to book in advance: tel: 985-8161

Special Interest Attractions

The world's largest seabed reservoir, **High Island**, is situated near the world's first, **Plover Cove**, in the Sai Kung Peninsula in the New Territories. High Island, which was completed in 1979, is capable of storing more than 273 million

Bird-watching is a serious business — as is choosing a good cage.

Day Trips

It's possible to leave Hong Kong for a day and visit either China or the Portuguese colony of Macau. Hydrofoils to **Macau** run several times a day. The 90-minute journey transports you to a tiny Mediterranean-style enclave with Chinese overtones just off the coast of China. Lovely tree-shaded lanes, charming old buildings, excellent food and wine and, of course, casinos (always packed at weekends when Hong Kong locals come over for gambling). Macau is really worth visiting and the contrast with Hong Kong is quite astonishing.

Telephone the **Macau Tourist Office** 3-677747 for further details.

China

Informationm on all trips and tours can be obtained from the **China Travel Service** at either 77 Queen's Road, Central or 27 Nathan Road in Kowloon. Inquire in person and take your passport. For short-time visitors, **Canton** can be reached by hydrofoil up the **Pearl River** for one-day trips, or there's a four-day tour including factories, temples, communes and all you ever wanted to know about life behind the "bamboo curtain."

Chinese Movie-Making

If you've ever wondered how kung-fu movies are made, the best idea is to write

in advance to the public relations department at either **Shaw Brothers** or **Golden Harvest**. The former is at 220 Clear Water Bay Road, Kowloon (tel: 3-291551) the latter at Hammer Hill Road, Kowloon (tel: 3-255241)

Chinese Cooking

Many classes and demonstrations. For information, call any of the following numbers: the **Hong Kong Electric Company** (5-7906536) the **Towngas Centre** (5-761535) and the **YWCA** cooking class (5-223101 ext 22.).

Trips to the countryside can include rides on a jet-foil, walks through deserted villages or watching the making of a kung-fu movie.

Travellers Tips

The Hong Kong Tourist Association (HKTA)

The free information brochures available from the HKTA branches listed below, include tremendous variety, such as details and lists of beaches, walks, of the different foods (even how to order **dim sum** and use chopsticks), the other islands, etc:

Buffer Hall, Kai Tak Airport, Kowloon
Star Ferry Concourse, Kowloon
Ground Floor, World Trade Centre, Causeway Bay, Hong Kong
Government Publications Centre, General Post office Building, Star Ferry, Hong Kong
35th Floor, **Connaught Centre**, Central, Hong Kong

The only telephone numbers necessary are 5-244191 and 3-671111 (office hours). The girls manning the phones do a remarkable job in answering any and all questions speedily and efficiently. The brochures and maps are a must; the answering service a great help.

Entry Requirements

Entry formalities are relatively simple: British subjects are admitted freely for up to six months and most other nationalities, including Americans, may enter without a visa provided their visit is for less than one month; visas valid for three months can be obtained from any British Consulate.

Health

HEALTH DOCUMENTS
A valid Certificate of Vaccination against smallpox is *not* required unless you visited a smallpox area in preceeding 14 days; likewise vaccination against cholera, unless arriving from an infected area.

DOCTORS
Consult the Yellow Pages of the telephone book under "Physicians and Surgeons." Fees for office calls range around $50 and home or hotel calls average $150.

HOSPITALS
Casualty wards for emergency accidents are open 24-hours a day at Queen Elizabeth Hospital, Wylie Road, Kowloon (tel: 3-840111) and Queen Mary Hospital, Pokfulam Road, Hong Kong (tel: 5-873873). The Hong Kong Adventist Hospital, 40 Stubbs Road, Hong Kong (tel: 5-746211) operates an out-patients clinic Sunday till Friday noon, and provides 24-hour emergency dental service.

WATER
Completely safe to drink.

CUSTOMS
You may bring into Hong Kong free of duty: Tobacco - 200 cigarettes or 50 cigars or 1/2 lb. tobacco. Liquor - one quart bottle. Cosmetics — cosmetics containing alcohol (perfume, lotions, etc.) in reasonable quantities in opened bottles for personal use. Firearms (personal property such as revolvers, rifles, etc.) must be declared and handed into custody until departure. But you may bring in your car for personal use, free of duty. All drivers with a valid overseas driving licence can drive in Hong Kong for a maximum period of one year. A motor insurance policy (third party insurance) is required.

Climate and Clothing

Spring, — March-April; jackets or sweaters; umbrella; wet and misty; Summer, May-August; short sleeves, cottons, a sweater (fierce air-conditioning); umbrella; hot, humid and rainy; Autumn, September-November; short sleeves, light sweater or jacket; most pleasant time of year. Typhoons, when they occur, can be expected from May to October. Winter, — December-February; suits, light woollens and sometimes overcoats; usually dry, sunny and cold.

Electricity

The voltage is 200V, 50 cycles. Electric razor points (generally with multi-fittings) are available in all hotels.

Population

The total latest population estimate of Hong Kong at August 1979 was 4,900,000, of which over 98 percent are Chinese — predominantly Cantonese. Round number estimates place the remainder as follows: 30,000 British Commonwealth subjects; 11,000 Americans; 3,800 Portuguese; 6,500 Japanese, 11,600 Filipinos; plus a few thousand other nationalities which only number a couple of hundred each.

Tipping

Tipping is an established practice in Hong Kong, but not mandatory. Baggage porters and bellhops expect to receive $2.00 a suitcase. Taxi-drivers who are pleasant get around 50¢ from locals, nothing if they're not. Nearly all restaurants include a 10 percent service charge to the bill and the local custom is to leave small change only.

A chair on the street is a poor substitute for sun and fresh air.

The Telephone

Kowloon telephone numbers have a "3" prefix (not dialled within Kowloon. **Hong Kong Island** telephone numbers have a "5" prefix (not dialled on Hong Kong. **New Territories** telephone numbers have a "12" prefix (not dialled in the New Territories). Telephone calls are free if made from private phones. Calls made from public telephones (usually in red or pink) cost 50¢ for local calls.

USEFUL TELEPHONE NUMBERS

Hong Kong Tourist Association
5-244191

Ambulance Service
5-245111

Hospital (Government)
5-468121

Fire Department
5-240024

Police Department
5-234011 or 999

Post Office
5-2671111

Kai Tak Airport
3-820211

Department of Immigration
5-436374

Directory Enquiries
108

International Calls
100

EMERGENCY (Police, Fire or Ambulance)
999

OVERSEAS CALLS/CABLES

Hotels can make arrangements, or else go to one of the Cable & Wireless Offices: New Mercury House (tel: 5-283111, 8 am-12 midnight); Ocean Terminal (tel: 3-664063, 7.30 am-midnight); Mercury House (tel: 5-237439, 24 hours service daily); Lee Gardens (tel: 5-770577, 10 am-1pm/2pm-6pm Monday to Friday, 10am-3pm Saturday, closed on Sunday; Kai Tak Airport (tel: 3-8297914, 8.30 am-10pm Monday to Saturday, 12 noon-7pm Sunday.

Airlines with Offices in Central District

Air France (AF)
21st Floor, Alexandra House
Tel: 5-223131

Air India (AI)
H.K. Hilton Hotel Arcade
Tel: 5-222131

Air New Zealand (TE)
G/F., Alexandra House,
Tel: 5-775023

Air Niugini (PX)
1001 Lane Crawford Hse.
Tel: 5-242151

China National Aviation Corporation (CA)
G/F Gloucester Tower
Tel: 211314

Korean Airlines (KE)
G/F., St. George's Bldg.
Tel: 5-235177

Lufthansa German Airlines (LH)
G/F., Prince's Bldg.
Tel: 5-242181

Could the fruit of 3000 years of civilization be sitting on these shelves?

Malaysian Airline System (MH)
21 Swire House, Chater Rd.
Tel: 5-252321

Alia Royal Jordanian Airline (RJ)
Rm. 2410-2411 Realty Bldg.
Tel: 266767

Alitalia (AZ)
H.K. Hilton Hotel Arcade
Tel: 5-237041

British Airways (BA)
G/F., Alexandra House
Tel: 5-775023

Canadian Pacific (CP)
Swire House, Chater Rd.
Tel: 248161

Cathay Pacific (CX)
G/F., Swire House
Tel: 250011

China Air Lines (CI)
St. George's Bldg.
Tel: 5-243011

Garuda (GA)
7-C Fu House, Ice House St.
Tel: 5-225033

Japan Airlines (JL)
P & O Bldg., Connaught Rd.
Tel: 5-245011

KLM Royal Dutch Airlines(KL)
Fu House, Ice House St.
Tel: 220081

Northwest Orient Airlines (NW)
St. George's Bldg.
Tel: 249261

Pan American (PA)
M/F. Alexandra House
Tel: 5-231111

Philippine Airlines (PR)
Swire House, Chater Rd.
Tel: 5-227010

Qantas Airways (QF)
G/F., Swire House
Tel: 229131

Scandinavian Airlines System (SK)
New Henry Hse, Des Voeux Rd.
Tel: 5-257051

Singapore Airlines (SQ)
G/F., Kayamally Bldg.
Tel: 5-253111

Swissair (SR)
New Henry House, Des Voeux Rd.
Tel: 5-226135

Thai International (TG)
New Henry House, Des Voeux Rd.
Tel: 5-257051

United Airlines (UA)
3/F., St. George's Bldg.
Tel: 5-226123

Hotels

Name two of the best hotels in Asia — The Peninsula and The Mandarin. Name the hotel chains — Hilton, Hyatt, Sheraton, Holiday Inn etc. Name the guest houses like the YMCA and YWCA. Hong Kong has them all. All are airconditioned and have modern amenities and are of an extremely high standard. Complaints are few, but if you encounter any difficulties you can contact the **Hong Kong Hotels Association** for advice or assistance. Telephone: 5-765324.

Hotel occupancy rates average 89 per cent yearly, consequently advance reservations are always necessary. You are also advised to **reconfirm** your booking.

Hotel representatives will meet expected guests at the airport. Transport is provided free of charge or at a resonable sum. Taxis are also stationed outside the airport, or you may use the Airport Coach Service No. 200 and No. 201, which calls at most of the hotels on Hong Kong Island and Kowloon peninsula. The fare is HK$4.00 and HK$2.50 respectively. It is necessary to tender the exact amount.

HONG KONG ISLAND HOTELS

Caravelle Hotel
84-86 Morrison Hill Road Happy Valley
5-754455

Excelsior Hotel
New Hoi Pong Road Causeway Bay
5-767365

Furama Hotel
1 Connaught Rd. Central
5-255111

Hong Kong Cathay Hotel
17 Tung Lo Wan Rd. Casueway Bay
5-778211

Harbour Hotel
116-122 Gloucester Rd. Wanchai
5-748211

Hilton Hotel
2A Queen's Rd. Central
5-233111

Island Hotel
1 Great George St. Causeway Bay
5-7902021

Lee Gardens Hotel
Hysan Avenue Causeway Bay
5-767211

Luk Kwok Hotel
67 Gloucester Rd. Wanchai
5-270721

Mandarin Hotel
5 Connaught Rd, Central
5-220111

Plaza Hotel
310 Gloucester Rd. Causeway Bay
7901021

Repulse Bay Hotel
109 Repulse Bay Rd. Repulse Bay
5-92211

Singapore Hotel
41-49 Hennessy Rd. Wanchai
5-272721

*The Peninsula Hotel's majestic lobby
evokes old colonial splendour.*

KOWLOON HOTELS

Ambassador Hotel
Nathan/4 Middle Road Tsim Sha Tsui
3-666321

Astor Hotel
11 Carnavon Rd. Tsim Sha Tsui
3-667261

Bangkok Hotel
2-12 Pilkem St. Yaumati
3-679181

Carlton Hotel
4-1/2 Miles Tai Po Rd.
3-866222

Chung Hing Hotel
380 Nathan Rd. Yaumati
3-887001

Empress Hotel
17-19 Chatham Road Tsim Sha Tsui
3-660211

First Hotel
206 Portland St. Mongkok
3-305211

Fortuna Court
2-4 Chi Woo St. Yaumati
3-304321

Fortuna Hotel
355 Nathan Rd. Yaumati
3-851011

Fuji Hotel
140-142 Austin Rd. Tsim Sha Tsui
3-678111

Galaxie Hotel
30 Pak Hoi St. Yaumati
3-307211

Grand Hotel
14 Carnarvon Rd. Tsim Sha Tsui
3-669331

Holiday Inn-Golden Mile
50 Nathan rd. Tsim Sha Tsui
3-693111

Holiday Inn-Harbour View
Ching Yee Rd., East Tsim Sha Tsui
3-2716238

Hong Kong Hotel
3 Canton Rd. Tsim Sha Tsui
3-676011

Hyatt Regency
67 Nathan Rd. Tsim Sha Tsui
3-662321

Imperial Hotel
32-34 Nathan Rd. Tsim Sha Tsui
3-662201

International Hotel
33 Cameron Rd. Tsim Sha Tsui
3-663381

King's Hotel
473 Nathan Rd. Yaumati
3-301281

Merlin Hotel
2 Hankow Rd. Tsim Sha Tsui
3-667211

Miramar Hotel
134 Nathan Rd. Tsim Sha Tsui
3-681111

Nathan Hotel
378 Nathan Rd. Yaumati
3-885141

New World Hotel
22 Salisbury Rd. Tsim Sha Tsui
3-694111

Park Hotel
61-65 Chatham Rd. Tsim Sha Tsui
3-661371

Pearl Island
17-1/2 Miles, Castle Peak Rd, N.T.
12-808111

Penninsula Hotel
Salisbury Rd. Tsim Sha Tsui
3-666251

Regent Hotel
Salisbury Rd., Tsim Sha Tsui
3-7211211

Shangri La
Ching Yee Rd., East Tsim Sha Tsui
3-7212111

Shamrock Hotel
223 Nathan Rd. Tsim Sha Tsui
3-666251

Sheraton Hotel
20 Nathan Rd. Tsim Sha Tsui
3-691111

Hostles and Guest Houses

HONG KONG ISLAND

Y.W.C.A.
1 Macdonnell Rd.
5-223101

KOWLOON

Chung King House
40 Nathan Rd. Tsim Sha Tsui
3-665362

International
40 Nathan Rd. Tsim Sha Tsui
3-664256

Washington Guest House
15A Austin Ave. Tsim Sha Tsui
3-690177

Y.W.C.A.
5 Man Fuk Road Waterloo Road Hill
3-039211

There is a real woman under this mask-like attire.

Y.M.C.A.
Salisbury Rd. Tsim Sha Tsui
3-692211

Y.M.C.A. Int'l House
23 Waterloo Rd. Yaumati
3-319111

NEW HOTEL DEVELOPMENTS
1981/82

Harbour City Hotel Project (opening April 1981)

Marco Polo (opening February 1982)
3-676011

Regal Airport Hotel (opening late 1981)
5-5431499

Regal Meridien Hotel (opening early 1982)
5-5431499

Royal Garden Hotel (opening December 1981)
5-214138

All telephone numbers listed above are pre-opening office numbers.

Cinemas/Movies

Movies are normally shown at 2.30 pm; 5.30 pm; 7.30 pm; 9.30 pm and cost on average $9.00 for Back Stalls (orchestra) and $11.00 for the Loge & Dress Circle (balcony). Programmes change with little notice so it is best to phone or consult daily newspapers for the latest programmes. Seats are all reserved and can be booked up to one day in advance.

HONG KONG ISLAND THEATRES

Cathay, 125 Wanchai Road.
5-724745

Hoover, 64 Yee Woo Street.
5-762371

Imperial, Wood Road.
5-722883

Isis, 7 Moreton Terrace.
5-773496

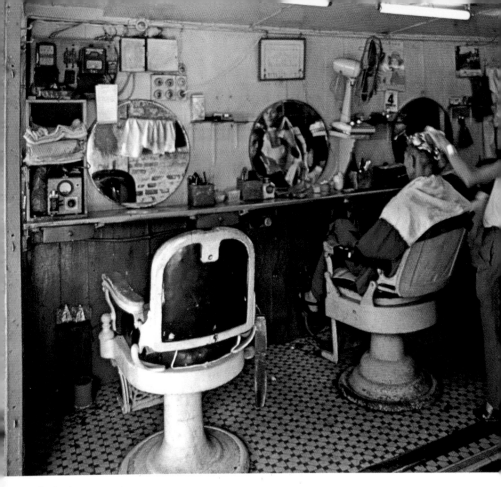

Jade, Paterson Street.
5-778117

King's, 34 Queen's Road.
5-225313

Lee, 27 Percival Street.
5-776319

Nan Yang, 23 Tin Lok Lane.
5-737388

New York, Hennessy Road.
5-763340

Oriental, 1 Fleming Road.
5-724907

Palace, 280 Gloucester Road.
5-7651679

Park, 180 Tunglowan Road.
5-705454

Pearl, Paterson Street.
5-776351

President, Jaffe Road.
5-761937

Queen's, 37 Queen's Road.
5-227036

State, 289 King's Road.
5-706241.

KOWLOON THEATRES

Empress, Sai Yeung Choi Street.
3-809570

Golden Harvest, 23 Jordan Road.
3-857151

Personal grooming needs can be satisfied in many ways.

Hollywood, 610 Soy Street.
3-841144

Liberty, 26E Jordan Road.
3-663783

London, 219 Nathan Road.
3-661056

Majestic, 334 Nathan Road.
3-847115

M2, 6-22 Saigon Street.
3-841199

Ocean, Harbour Centre.
3-678091

Rex, Portland/Argyle Streets.
3-963110

Royal, 748 Nathan Road.
3-945300

Sands, 17 Hankow Road.
3-663883

Washington, 92 Parkes Street.
3-310405.

Language

A large percentage of the Chinese population can speak English as well as their own dialect so it is no problem to ask for directions or assistance in urban sections. Of the many Chinese dialects, Cantonese is naturally the most prevalent, but Shanghainese and Mandarin plus several dozen others are also spoken.

Business Contacts

Hong Kong Trade Development Council
3/F., Connaught Centre, Central District.
Hours: 9 am/12.30 pm; 1.30 pm/5 pm
Mon-Fri, 9 am/12.30 pm Saturday.
Tel: 5-257151

The Hong Kong General Chamber of Commerce
902 Swire House, Central District.
Hours: 9 am/12.30 pm; 1.30 pm/5 pm
Mon-Fri, 9 am/12 noon Saturday.
Tel: 5-237177

The Chinese General Chamber of Commerce
24 Connaught Road, 7/F., Central District.
Hours: 9 am/1 pm; 2 pm/5 pm Mon-Fri,
9 am/1 pm Saturday.
Tel: 5-256385

Hong Kong Exporters Association
1625 Star House (near Star Ferry), Kowloon.
Hours: 9 am/1 pm; 2 pm/5 pm Mon-Fri,
9 am/12 noon Saturday.
Tel: 3-677422

Trade Industry & Customs Department
Ocean Centre, Kowloon.
Hours: 8.15 am/12.30 pm; 1.30/5.15 pm
Mon-Fri, 9 am/12 noon Saturday.
Tel: 3-677422

Trade Marks Registry
1608 Melbourne Plaza, Central District.
Hours: 8.40 am/12.40 pm; 1.40/5.10 pm
Mon-Fri, 8.40 am/12.40 pm Saturday.
Tel: 5-229557

Secretariat For Home Affairs
10/F., International Building, Central Distric.
Hours: 9 am/1 pm; 2 pm/5.30 pm Mon-Fri, 9 am/ noon Saturday.
Tel: 5-452091

Inland Revenue Department
9/F., West Wing, Central Government Offices.
Hours: 8.30 am/13.30 pm; 1.30/5 pm
Mon-Fri, 9 am/12.30 pm Saturday.
Tel: 5-222151

Immigration Department
14/F., International Building, Central District.
Hours: 9 am/5 pm Mon-Fri, 9 am/12.30 Saturday.
Tel: 5-456065

Labour Department
Lee Gardens, 2/F., Hysan Avenue, Causeway Bay.
Hours: 9 am/1 pm; 2 pm/5.30 pm Mon-Fri, 9 am/12 noon Saturday.
Tel: 5-778271

American Chamber of Commerce
Swire House, Central District.

Hours: 9 am/12.30 pm; 2 pm/5 pm Mon-
Fri, 9 am/12.30 Saturday.
Tel: 5-259215

Clubs & Associations

Aberdeen Boat Club (5-524687)
Aero Club of Hong Kong (3-020221)
Alliance Francaise
(5-277845 or 3-693257)
American Chamber of Commerce
(5-259215)
American Club (5-244013)
American Women's Association
(5-272961)
Archaeological Society (3-671124)
Asiatic Society (5-260031)
Australian Association (5-251593)
Autombile Association (5-743394)
Badminton Association (3-663824)
Bird Watching Society
(5-468161 Zoology Department, HK
University)
Bridge (Contract) Association
(5-702251)
British Council (Kowloon Office &
Library 3-660664)
Canadian Club (5-262011)
Catholic Club (5-237438)
China Fleet Club (5-270621)
Cricket Club (5-746266)
Deutsches Haus (German Club)
(5-438349)
Fencing (Amateur) Association
(P.O. Box 4981)
Filipino Club (3-888193)
Football Association (5-7905522)
Foreign Correspondents' Club
(5-237734)
**The Gemmological Association of Hong
Kong** (3-666006)
Goethe Institute (5-451173)
Golf Club (5-232340)
Hash House Harriers (5-252161)
Hong Kong Club (5-223187)
Hong Kong Darts Association
(5-746785)
Hong Kong Rugby Football Union
(5-749794)
Indian Association (5-225596)
Indonesia Club (5-274974)
Japanese Club (5-243247)

Jaycees International (5-488913)
Jewish Recreation Club (5-229872)
Jockey Club (5-7906321)
Kiwanis Club (5-240018)
Korean Club (5-770454)
Ladies Recreation Club (5-220151)
Lawn Tennis Association (5-797021)
Lions Club (5-221836)
Mountaineering Club (5-760727)
New Zealand Society (12-908640)
Rotary Club (5-232342)
Round Tables in Hong Kong (5-249021)
Sea Dragon Skin Diving Club (5-747951)
St. Andrew's Society (P.O. Box 690)
St. David's Society of Hong Kong
(P.O. Box NP-4660)
St. George's Society (5-220086)
St. Patrick's Society (P.O. Box 615)
Under Water Club (5-754343)
United Nations Association (5-220881)
Y.M.C.A. (3-692211)
Y.W.C.A. (5-223101)
Yacht Club (5-761851)

Consulates/Visas

America
26 Garden Road.
Hours: 8.30/10.30 am & 1.30/3.30 pm
Mon-Fri.
5-239011

Australia
10/F., Connaught Centre.
Hours: 9.30 am/1.00 pm; 2.00/4.30 pm
Mon-Fri.
5-227171

Austria
Room 2201 Wang Kee Building.
Hours: 9.00 am/12.00 noon Mon-Fri.
5-239716

Belgium
1803 World Trade Centre.
Hours: 9.00 am/12.00 noon; 3.00/4.00
pm Mon-Fri.
5-7907321

Little by little the far sides of the harbour are hidden by growing sky-lines.

Brazil
1107 Shell House.
Hours: 9.30 am/1.30 pm Mon-Fri.
5-257002

Canada
14th & 15th Floors, Asian House.
Hours: 8.30 am/12.30 pm; 1.30/5.00 pm
Mon-Fri.
5-282222

China, People's Republic of
77 Queen's Road.
Hours: 9.00 am/1,00 pm; 2.00/5.00
Mon-Sat.
5-259121

Denmark
1302 Chartered Bank Building.
Hours: 10.00 am/12.00 noon; 2.00/4.00
pm Mon-Fri.
5-221585

Egypt
20 MacDonnel Road.
Hours: 9.00 am/12.00 noon Mon-Fri,
9.00 am/11.30 am Saturday.
5-244174

Finland
1409 Hutchison House.
Hours: 10.00 am/12.30 pm; 2.30/4.30
pm Mon-Fri.
5-244892

France
1208 Hang Seng Bank Building.
Hours: 9.30 am/1.00 pm Mon-Fri.
5-224096

Germany
12/F., Realty Building.
Hours: 9.00 am/12.00 noon Mon-Fri.
5-221031

Greece
1702A Alexandra House.
Hours: 9.00 am/1.00 pm; 2.00/5.00 pm
Mon-Fri, 9.00 am/1.00 pm Saturday.
5-243419

Hong Kong Immigration Department
15/F., International Building.
Hours: 9.00 am/5.00 pm Mon-Fri, 9.00
am/12.00 noon Saturday.
5-456065

India
303 AIA Building.
Hours: 9.00 am/1.00 pm; 2.00/3.00 pm
Mon-Fri.
5-756362

Indonesia
6-8 Keswick Street.
Hours: 10.00 a.m./12.30 pm; 2.30/4.30
pm Mon-Fri.
5-7904421

Iran
Room 1202-3 Gammon House.
Hours: 9.00 am/1,00 pm; 2.00/5.00 pm
Mon-Fri, 9.00 am/12.00 noon Saturday.
5-241109

Irish Republic
8/F., Prince's Building.
Hours: 9.00 am/12.30 pm; 2.30/5.00 pm
Non-Fri, 9.00 am/12.30 pm Saturday.
5-231011

Israel
1122 Prince's Building.
Hours: 10.00 am/1.00 pm; 2.00/4.00 pm
Mon-Fri.
5-220177

And again the sun sets over a city which changes its face every day.

Italy
801 Hutchison House.
Hours: 9.30 am/1.00 pm; 2.30/4.30 pm
Mon-Fri, 9.30 am/12.00 noon Saturday.
5-220033

Japan
24/F., Gammon House.
Hours: 9.30 am/12.00 noon; 2.00/4.00
pm Mon. Tues. Thurs. Fri, 9.30/12.00
noon Wednesday.
5-221184

Jordan
504 Lansing House.
Hours: 9.30 am/12.30 pm; 2.30/4.30 pm
Mon-Fri, 9.30 am/12.00 noon Saturday.
5-221507

Korea
Korea Centre Building 3/F.
Hours: 10.00 am/12.00 noon; 2.00/4.00
pm Mon-Fri, 10.00 am/12.00 noon
Saturday.
5-430224

Malaysia
21/F., Permanent Comfort Building.
Hours: 9.00 am/12.30 pm; 2.00/5.00 pm
Mon-Fri.
5-457156

Mexico
Room 2704 International Building.
Hours 9.00 am/1.00 pm Mon-Fri.
5-454245

Netherlands
Room 1505 Central Building.
Hours: 9.00 am/1.00 pm; 2.00/5.35 pm
Mon-Fri.
5-258095

Norway
502 AIA Building.
Hours: 9.30 am/12.30 pm; 2.00/4.30 pm
Mon-Fri.
5-749253

Pakistan
Room 307-8 Asian House.
Hours: 9.30 am/1.00 pm; 2.00/5.00 pm
Mon-Fri, 9.30 am/1.00 pm Saturday;
5-274623

Philippines
8/F., Hang Lung Bank Building.

Hours: 9.00 am/3.00 pm Mon-Fri.
5-7908823

Portugal
1405-12 Central Building.
Hours: 9.00 a,/3.00 pm Mon-Fri.
5-225789

Singapore
19/F., Wang Kee Building.
Hours: 9.30 am/12.00 pm; 2.00/5.00 pm
Mon-Fri.
5-247091

South Africa
701 AIA Building.
Hours 9.00 am/12.30 pm; 2.00/5.00 pm
Mon-Fri.
5-743351

Spain
1404-5 Melbourne Plaza Building.
Hours: 9.00 am/1.00 pm Mon-Fri.
5-253041

Sweden
1107 Hang Seng Bank Building.
Hours: 9.00 am/1.00 pm Mon-Fri.
5-227125

Switzerland
403 Shell House.
Hours: 9.30 am/12.00 noon; 2.00/4.00
pm Mon-Fri.
5-227147

Taiwan (Chung Wah Travel)
1009 Tak Shing House.
Hours: 9.00 am/12.30 pm; 2.00/5.00 pm
Mon-Fri, 9.00 am/12.00 noon Saturday.
5-258315

Thailand
221-226 Gloucester Road.
Hours: 10.00 am/12.00 noon; 2.30/4.30
pm Mon-Fri.
5-742201

Turkey
1303 Wing On Centre.
Hours: 9.00 am/12.00 noon; 2.00/5.00
pm Mon-Fri, 9.00 am/12.00 noon
Saturday.
5-442252 Ext 450.

Index